D0733520

The Applause Libretto Library Series

MEMPHIS

The Complete Book and Lyrics of the Broadway Musical

Book and Lyrics by Joe DiPietro

Music and Lyrics by David Bryan

APPLAUSE
THEATRE & CINEMA BOOKS

AN IMPRINT OF HAL LEONARD CORPORATION

Published in 2011 by Applause Theatre & Cinema Books
An Imprint of Hal Leonard Corporation
7777 West Bluemound Road
Milwaukee, WI 53213

Trade Book Division Editorial Offices
33 Plymouth St., Montclair, NJ 07042

Printed in the United States of America

Book design by Mark Lerner
Photos by Joan Marcus

Library of Congress Cataloging-in-Publication Data

Bryan, David, 1962-
  [Memphis. Libretto]
  Memphis : the complete book and lyrics of the Broadway musical / book and lyrics by Joe DiPietro ; music and lyrics by David Bryan.
    p. cm.
  ISBN 978-1-55783-771-4 (pbk.)
  1. Musicals--Librettos. I. DiPietro, Joe. II. Title.
  ML50.B8998M46 2011
  782.1'40268--dc22
                              2011005688

ISBN 978-1-55783-771-4

www.applausepub.com

FOREWORD

The Tony Award–winning Broadway musical *Memphis*, set in the 1950s, bursts with the energy of the newly minted music called rock 'n' roll. The times were starting to change with the Supreme Court's school-desegregation decision in *Brown vs. the Board of Education*, followed by the Montgomery bus boycott, which sparked the civil rights movement. Even music had been segregated, with black artists confined to "race" music radio stations. But the driving beat ultimately won out and became rock 'n' roll, a term that deejay Alan Freed allegedly invented. The bland pop music of Perry Como and Patti Page gave way to the sensually charged sounds of Elvis Presley, Bill Haley, Chuck Berry, and Little Richard.

In *Memphis*, set amid the racially explosive background of the segregated South, Huey Calhoun, a rebellious white boy, gets up the guts to drop in at Delray's jumping Beale Street club. As the lyric of "Underground" says: "Ain't no white folks here 'cause they too damn scared!" At the club, Huey calls the sounds "the music of my soul" and his single-minded devotion to that beat finally wins him a deejay spot playing music on a white radio station. Its teenage listeners, fed up with silly novelty songs and dull crooners, jump on Huey's bandwagon to make him the number-one deejay in the city. White and black teens dancing to the same beat and blasting the same songs from their transistor radios started to realize that maybe they weren't so different after all.

At Delray's, Huey falls hard for a dynamic black singer named Felicia Farrell. Felicia and Huey carry on an affair that brings trouble down on their heads in segregated Memphis, but their journey together gives us unique insight into the struggles for racial equality nearly sixty years ago.

Memphis, with book and lyrics by Joe DiPietro and music and lyrics by David Bryan, gives a strong voice to the exuberance, energy, and vitality of the early days of rock 'n' roll. Huey personifies all the disc jockeys of the time who changed America's listening habits by pushing this new music. For those too young to remember the fifties, it's hard to understand how upstanding citizens could campaign against rock 'n' roll as the devil's music. Now every wedding band plays the tunes. *Memphis* helps remind us how far as a nation we have come—from segregated drinking fountains to Barack Obama in the White House.

—Loraine Alterman Boyle

Originally produced in New York City by Junkyard Dog Productions, Sue Frost, Randy Adams, and Kenny Alhadeff

Originally Presented on Broadway by Junkyard Dog Productions, Barbara and Buddy Freitag, Marleen and Kenny Alhadeff, Latitude Link, Jim and Susan Blair, Demos Bizar Entertainment, Land Line Productions, Apples and Oranges Productions, Dave Copley, Dancap Productions, Inc., Alex and Katya Lukianov, Tony Ponturo, 2 Guys Productions and Richard Winkler

In association with

Lauren Doll, Eric and Marsi Gardiner, Linda and Bill Potter, Broadway Across America (John Gore, CEO; Thomas B. McGrath, Chairman; Beth Williams, COO & Head of Production), Jocko Productions, Patty Baker, Dan Frishwasser, Bob Bartner/Scott and Kaylin Union, Loraine Boyle/Chase Mishkin, Remmel T. Dickinson/Memphis Orpheum Group and ShadowCatcher Entertainment/Vijay and Sita Vashee

MUSICAL NUMBERS

Act 1

"Underground"	Delray, Felicia, and Clubgoers
"The Music of My Soul"	Hucy, Felicia, and Clubgoers
"Scratch My Itch"	Wailin' Joe and Customers
"Ain't Nothin' But a Kiss"	Felicia
"Hello, My Name Is Huey"	Huey
"Everybody Wants to Be Black on Saturday Night"	Trio
"That's Not Possible"	Buck Wiley, Mr. Simmons, Bobby, and Teenagers
"Everybody Wants to Be Black on Saturday Night 2"	Trio and Teenagers
"Make Me Stronger"	Felicia, Huey, Gladys, and Choir
"Colored Woman"	Felicia and Huey
"Someday"	Felicia and Backups
"She's My Sister"	Delray and Huey
"Ain't Nothin' but a Kiss Reprise"	Felicia
"Radio"	Huey and Company
"Say a Prayer"	Gator and Company

Act 2

"Crazy Little Huey"	Huey and Dancers
"Big Love"	Bobby
"Love Will Stand When All Else Falls"	Felicia and Backups
"Stand Up"	Felicia, Huey, Delray, Gator, and Company
"Change Don't Come Easy"	Gladys, Delray, Gator, and Bobby
"Scratch My Itch Reprise"	Wailin' Joe
"Tear Down the House"	Huey and Dancers
"Love Will Stand When All Else Falls Reprise"	Huey and Felicia
"Memphis Lives in Me"	Huey and Company
"Steal Your Rock 'n' Roll"	Felicia, Huey, and Company

ACT 1

SCENE 1

Prologue

A disc jockey booth.

[*Lights up on* WHITE DISC JOCKEY *speaking into a mike.*]

WHITE DISC JOCKEY   And welcome back, my friends, to WHTE, right smack in the center of your radio dial. And we've just ended 1951 as your *number*-one station in Memphis, playing you the most popular music from all across the U.S. of . . .

[*Blackout. Music hit. We hear and see a radio dial quickly being turned to its outer range. Lights flash up on a* BLACK DISC JOCKEY.]

BLACK DISC JOCKEY   What's shakin', brothers and sisters. I'm glad you found us way up here on the dial! And even though we only reachin' 'bout a mile across Downtown Memphis—

[*Music hit.*]

We got us the jumpin'est, jivin'est music in town!

[*Music hit.*]

And it's Saturday night, meanin' the party's at my favorite Beale Street Juke Joint—Delray's!

[*The disc jockey booth disappears. We are in Delray's underground juke joint. DELRAY, the owner of the club, presides.*]

"UNDERGROUND"

DELRAY   TIME TO LOSE THE DAY, TIME TO HEAD TO BEALE,
WHERE THE RHYTHM IS HOT AND THE MUSIC IS REAL.
YOU CAN DO WITHOUT LOVE, YOU CAN SWEAR OFF THE BOOZE . . .
BUT EVERYONE ALIVE NEEDS TO SING THE BLUES,
SO TIME TO RAISE SOME HELL AND GET ON DOWN

DELRAY and CLUBGOERS   WE GOIN' DOWN, DOWN UNDERGROUND

MALE CLUBGOERS   DOWN UNDERGROUND, DOWN UNDER

DELRAY and CLUBGOERS   WE GOIN' DOWN, DOWN, DOWN, JUST TO HEAR THAT SOUND

FEMALE CLUBGOERS   WE GOIN' DOWN, WE GOIN'

DELRAY and CLUBGOERS   WE'RE GONNA DANCE SO CLOSE, FEEL MY BREATH ON YOUR SKIN

DELRAY   AIN'T QUITE HEAVEN BUT THE CLOSEST I BEEN

DELRAY and CLUBGOERS   WE GOIN' DOWN, DOWN UNDERGROUND

DELRAY   FIRST WE HEARD IT IN CHURCH

CLUBGOERS   AMEN!

DELRAY   THEN WE ADDED SOME GIN

CLUBGOERS   YE AH AH

DELRAY   THEN WE TOOK IT DOWN HERE

MALE CLUBGOERS   WE TOOK IT DOWN HERE

DELRAY and CLUBGOERS   AND ADDED SOUL WITH SIN!

DELRAY and CLUBGOERS   GONNA JUMP AND JIVE LIKE A DEMON POSSESSED

DELRAY   THE DEVIL'S IN THE MUSIC AND THE MUSIC
IS BLEST

DELRAY and CLUBGOERS   WE GOIN' DOWN WHERE
PARADISE IS FOUND.
WE GOIN' DOWN, DOWN UNDERGROUND

MALE CLUBGOERS   DOWN UNDERGROUND, DOWN
UNDER

DELRAY and CLUBGOERS   WE GOIN' DOWN, DOWN,
DOWN, JUST TO BURN THAT SOUND

MALE CLUBGOERS   DOWN UNDERGROUND, DOWN
UNDER

DELRAY   GONNA DO SOME THINGS THAT YOU
NEVER DARED.
AIN'T NO WHITE FOLKS HERE—'CAUSE THEY TOO
DAMN SCARED!

DELRAY and CLUBGOERS   WE GOIN' DOWN, DOWN
UNDERGROUND

[FELICIA *enters.*]

FELICIA   Here I am!

DELRAY   Baby girl, where you been? Didn't see you all day!

FELICIA   Ah, don't you know by now, big brother—there ain't no daytime on Beale Street, only nighttime!

[CROWD *reacts.*]

Now get outta my way and lemme sing my song. Hey, ya'll! Two-three-four!

[FELICIA *takes the stage.*]

FELICIA   MY BROTHER RUNS MY LIFE, MY BROTHER OWNS THIS BAR!

DELRAY   That's right—

FELICIA   HE WON'T LET ME BE TILL HE MAKES ME A STAR!
HE GIVES ME THIS MIKE, MAKES ME SING ALL I CAN,
JUST CAN'T HAVE NO FUN OR TALK TO NO MAN.
I WANNA PAINT THE TOWN, BUT WITH HIM AIN'T NO FOOLIN' AROUND! WOAH!
WE GOIN' DOWN, DOWN UNDERGROUND.

MALE CLUBGOERS   DOWN UNDERGROUND, DOWN UNDER

FELICIA   WE GOIN' DOWN, DOWN, DOWN, JUST TO HEAR THAT SOUND

CLUBGOERS   WE GOIN' DOWN, WE GOIN'

FELICIA and CLUBGOERS   GONNA GROPE AND GRIND, GONNA HOLD ON TIGHT

FELICIA   GONNA FIND TRUE LOVE AT LEAST FOR TONIGHT

FELICIA and CLUBGOERS   WE GOIN' DOWN, DOWN UNDERGROUND

FELICIA   Woah! Come on, y'all!

[CLUBGOERS *dance up a storm.*]

DELRAY   IT'S A REVOLUTION OF THE HEART AND SOUL

FELICIA   IT'S HERE TO STAY, AIN'T NEVER GONNA GO!

DELRAY/FELICIA   IT'S A REBEL CRY THAT'S OUTTA CONTROL! IT'S THE BIRTH OF ROCK 'N' ROLL!

ALL   ROCK 'N' ROLL! ROCK 'N' ROLL! ROCK 'N' ROLL!

DELRAY/FELICIA   WE   GOIN'   DOWN,   DOWN UNDERGROUND

DELRAY   WE GOIN' DOWN! WE GOIN' DOWN !

FELICIA   WE GOIN' DOWN, DOWN, DOWN—GOTTA ROCK THAT SOUND!

DELRAY   WE'RE GONNA DANCE AND DRINK TILL THE WHISKEY'S ALL GONE

FELICIA   THEN PRAY THAT THE PREACHER FORGIVES US AT DAWN

ALL   WE GOIN' DOWN, DOWN UNDERGROUND

DELRAY/CLUBGOERS   WE GOIN' UNDERGROUND, WE GOIN' UNDERGROUND!

FELICIA   WE GOIN' UNDERGROUND!

DELRAY/CLUBGOERS   WE GOIN' UNDERGROUND!

FELICIA   WE GOIN' UNDERGROUND!

ALL   WE GOIN' UNDERGROUND!

[*Music buttons.* HUEY, *an eccentric, young white man, enters.*]

HUEY   [*A cappella.*] WE GOIN' DOWN, DOWN UNDER- GROUND . . . DOWN UNDER . . . DOWN UNDER . . .

[*To* GATOR.]

Hi there!

[GATOR *crosses away.*]

See you later! Hi there! Fantastical music, ain't it?

[*A beat.*]

My first time here.

DELRAY   Yeah, I know.

HUEY   Name's Calhoun, Huey Calhoun.

DELRAY   Delray Farrell, sir. This is my club. And if you don't mind me askin', why you here, sir?

HUEY   What do ya mean?

DELRAY   I mean, you notice anything different between you and everybody else, sir?

[*He glances around. A beat.*]

HUEY   No.

DELRAY   I just don't want no trouble, sir.

HUEY   And I don't wanna cause no trouble. And the name ain't "sir," it's Huey.

FELICIA   What my brother is tryin' to say, Huey—

DELRAY   Felicia!

FELICIA   This is Beale Street. We don't see many white folks 'round here, unless they officers of the law, we gotta slip 'em some cash. So maybe you should leave.

HUEY   Tell ya the truth, ma'am, I ain't never had the nerve to come in a club like this before. But I heard you singin' . . .

FELICIA   And?

HUEY   And I wanted to see if you looked as pretty as you sound.

CLUBGOER   Oh, shit—

CLUBGOER   Del, we're gonna head out.

[CLUBGOERS *ad lib and begin to leave.*]

HUEY   Hold on now! I'm just here 'cause I like the music.

DELRAY   Look, sir . . .

HUEY   The name's Huey—and I just like the music.

CLUBGOER   We'll see ya tomorrow, Delray—

DELRAY   Now don't everybody go—

FELICIA   You wanna stay, you better convince everyone else to.

HUEY   Delray! Lemme handle this, brother.

[HUEY *sits at the piano and plays a chord.* CLUBGOERS *stop.*]

"THE MUSIC OF MY SOUL"

WHEN I WAS A YOUNG BOY
MY DADDY SAT ME DOWN.
HE SAID, "SON, DON'T YOU NEVER GO
TO THE DARK SIDE OF TOWN."

DELRAY   This ain't helpin'.

[HUEY *crosses to the mike.*]

HUEY   "I'M TALKIN' DOWNTOWN MEMPHIS, SEE,
THAT'S WHERE THE BLACK FOLK PLAY."
AN' I SAID, "YES, SIR, DADDY!"
AND THEN I SNUCK DOWN ANYWAY!

SEE, NEVER WAS TAUGHT TO READ NONE,
NO, NEVER TAUGHT TO WRITE.
THE ONLY THING MY DADDY TAUGHT
WAS WHITE SHOULD STAY WITH WHITE.

BUT I HEARD IT THROUGH THE ALLEYS,
IT FLOATED ON THE BREEZE.
IT BURST OUT THROUGH THE DOORWAYS
AND KNOCKED ME TO MY KNEES!

IT BROKE DOWN ALL MY SENSES
YET MADE ME FEEL SO WHOLE.

SEE, I WAS LOST UNTIL I FOUND
THE MUSIC OF MY SOUL.
THE MUSIC OF MY SOUL.

Then one day my Daddy died.
And we laid him in his grave—

AND MY MAMA, SHE CRIED AND CRIED AND CRIED
AND PRAYED THAT HE BE SAVED

BUT ALL I FELT WAS PITY
FOR HE NEVER UNDERSTOOD—
HOW COULD PEOPLE BE SO BAD
THAT MADE ME FEEL SO GOOD?

IT WHIPPED RIGHT THROUGH MY BODY.
IT GRABBED ME BY THE HEART.

FELICIA IT SHOT UP FROM MY FINGERTIPS
AND TORE ME RIGHT APART!

HUEY/FELICIA IT BROKE DOWN ALL MY SENSES
YET MADE ME FEEL SO WHOLE.
AND I WILL LOVE IT TO THE DAY I DIE.

ALL THE MUSIC OF MY SOUL!

IT BROKE DOWN ALL MY SENSES
YET MADE ME FEEL SO WHOLE.
SEE, I WAS LOST UNTIL I FOUND

I WAS DEAF UNTIL I HEARD.

HUEY I'LL MAKE THIS WORLD COME AROUND TO

ALL THE MUSIC OF MY SOUL! THE MUSIC OF MY SOUL!

SCENE 2

Collins Department Store, a couple of weeks later.

[*The whites- only customers mill about.* MR. COLLINS *plays host.*]

MR. COLLINS Greetings, Mr. Wells, right fine to see you. Afternoon, Miss Simpson, got a nice sale on cutlery today.

[*Off stage, a loud crash.*]

[HUEY *enters, carrying a large box.*]

Calhoun, what the hell was that?!

HUEY I'm sorry, Mr. Collins, I was carrying this big ol' box of dishes and somehow it just slipped outta my hands and . . .

MR. COLLINS And broke into a million pieces!

[MR. COLLINS *angrily slaps the box, causing it to noisily crash to the floor.*]

HUEY   Actually, it was another box, sir, but—

[MR. COLLINS *looks ready to explode.*]

Mr. Collins! I know what you're gonna say! But just give me one last chance!

MR. COLLINS   Why in hell should I?!

HUEY   Well, to be honest with ya, sir, I have a little trouble keepin' jobs. And my mama's gonna have my hide if I lose this one, too.

MR. COLLINS   Boy, last week I gave you a last chance in the stockroom, and the week before I gave you a last chance in the cafeteria.

HUEY   But you never gave me a last chance in the record department!

MR. COLLINS   What?

HUEY   See, I got this idea, sir. You know how Clara plays a record from time to time. Well, she only plays maybe a few a day, and quite frankly, sir, they ain't good records. So what I was thinkin' was, see, what if I spin records all day! It'd be like listenin' to the radio 'ceptin' you can buy the records right then and there!

MR. COLLINS   Calhoun, that idea actually ain't stupid. All right, look here, I gotta get to the bank. By the time I get back—Clara, how many records we usually sell this time of day?

CLARA   Two or three, Mr. Collins.

MR. COLLINS   Calhoun, by the time I get back, if you don't sell at least four—no five!— records, you're fired for good!

HUEY   Five records?!

MR. COLLINS   And here's some smart advice, boy. Play that Perry Como. He's everybody's favorite.

[MR. COLLINS *exits.* HUEY *crosses to a small area with a record player and microphone.*]

HUEY   [*Into the mike.*] Hello, uh, hello, good shoppers. Name is Huey Calhoun. And I got this record here for you. Yes, sir, this here is, uh, everybody's favorite, Mr. Perry Como.

[PERRY COMO *appears*]

"SUMMER HEART"

PERRY COMO   LIKE A BREEZE YOU/YOU BLEW IN—

HUEY   Oh, that's good.

PERRY COMO   THROUGH THE TREES YOU/YOU FLEW IN—

HUEY   Everybody's favorite.

PERRY COMO   AND STOLE MY SUMMER HEART . . .

[HUEY *cuts off the record, and* PERRY COMO *vanishes.*]

HUEY   Sorry folks, but Perry Como was puttin' me into a Perry coma!

[HUEY *puts on another record.*]

CLARA   Mr. Calhoun! What're you doing?!

[*Music starts.* WAILIN' JOE, *a wild rhythm & blues singer, appears.*]

"SCRATCH MY ITCH"

WAILIN' JOE   WOO! COME ON, BABY. NOW WON'T
YOU SCRATCH MY ITCH!
YOU GOT ME BOILING AT A BURNIN' FEVER PITCH!
I TRIED SOME LOVE CREAM. PUT SOME HONEY ON IT,
TOO!
BUT THE ONLY THING THAT CAN CURE MY ITCH IS
YOU!

COME ON, SCRATCH-SCRATCH-SCRATCH
SCRATCH-SCRATCH MY ITCH!
SCRATCH-SCRATCH-SCRATCH
SCRATCH-SCRATCH MY ITCH!

BABY, BABY, BABY
BABY, BABY, BABE
BABY, BABE,
YOU'RE GIVIN' ME A TWITCH!
SO SCRATCH MY ITCH!

[*Dance break, as the white customers can't help but give in to the new sound.*]

CUSTOMERS   SCRATCH-SCRATCH-SCRATCH-
SCRATCH-SCRATCH-SCRATCH

FEMALE CUSTOMERS	**MALE CUSTOMERS**
SCRATCH-SCRATCH-SCRATCH	BABY, BABY, BABY
SCRATCH-SCRATCH-SCRATCH	BABY, BABY, BABY
SCRATCH-SCRATCH-SCRATCH	BABY, BABY, BABY
SCRATCH-SCRATCH-SCRATCH	BABY, BABY, BABY

[MR. COLLINS *has entered; he can't believe his eyes.*]

MR. COLLINS   Stop!

[*Music and dancing immediately stops.*]

You're fired!

HUEY   But I was just trying to sell five records!

MR. COLLINS   And did you?!

HUEY   No, sir.

MR. COLLINS   I knew it! Get out!

HUEY   I sold twenty- nine.

MR. COLLINS   What?

HUEY   I sold twenty -nine records. And they was my own re-cords, so you owe me four dollars and ninety- five cents.

CLARA   It was race records, sir. He sold race records.

MR. COLLINS   Son, this is nigger music. And there ain't no niggers here. You will pack your things and go.

[MR. COLLINS *exits.* HUEY *glances over at the teenage girl, still lost in the music*]

TEENAGE GIRL   [*Introspective.*] SCRATCH-SCRATCH-SCRATCH-SCRATCH-SCRATCH MY ITCH . . .

HUEY   You really likin' this?

TEENAGE GIRL   Yes, sir.

[HUEY, *encouraged, rushes off.*]

SCENE 3

Delray's Night Club, that night. FELICIA *onstage. The party is going strong.*

"AIN'T NOTHIN' BUT A KISS"

FELICIA   YOU'RE A DOG AND BABY, I'M DOG -TIRED.
YOU'RE A DRUG, THE KIND THAT GETS ME WIRED.
I SHOULD SAY GOOD NIGHT BUT YOU GOT ME ALL
INSPIRED!

AIN'T NOTHIN' BUT A KISS
THAT SETS A GIRL ON FIRE
A SIMPLE LITTLE KISS
ALL LIPSTICK AND DESIRE
TAKE A TASTE OF THIS
AIN'T NOTHIN' BUT A KISS

Hit it, Vernon—

  [HUEY *enters. Music underscores.*]

HUEY   Hey, hey!

BOBBY   Evenin', Huey—

CLUBGOER   Huey, how's it goin'!

HUEY   Hey, Miss Felicia, your favorite customer has returned!

FELICIA   And since when is my favorite customer a pasty white boy?

HUEY   Well, I will be, once I get you on the radio.

FELICIA   The radio? Sugar, you know how a woman can tell when a man is lyin'?

HUEY   How?

FELICIA   He opens his mouth.

TAKE A TASTE OF THIS
AIN'T NOTHIN' BUT A KISS!

Go on, Chester, show me what you're working with! Ow!

[HUEY *crosses to* GATOR.]

HUEY   Hey, Gator, you think Miss Felicia's taken a likin' to me?

[GATOR *slides him a beer.*]

Ya know, Gator, for a bartender, you awfully quiet.

[FELICIA *crosses to the bar to get a drink.*]

FELICIA   When he was five, he seen his daddy get strung up right in front of his eyes. Nobody's heard him talk since.

HUEY He just stopped, huh?

FELICIA Sometimes, folks don't think there's anythin' left to say. But you don't seem to have that problem.

[*She crosses away back to the stage as* DELRAY *enters.*]

HUEY Hey, brother—

DELRAY Don't call me brother.

HUEY I was just tellin' your sister that I'm gonna take this music and do something with it.

DELRAY Take it? What do you mean, like, steal it?

HUEY I mean, take it and get it heard! It's the music of my soul, baby!

DELRAY It ain't the music of your soul, baby. It's the music of my soul. And my soul don't want your soul stealin' none of my music.

HUEY What you talkin' about, stealin'? I'm gonna spin this music on the radio. And I'm gonna get your sister on the radio, too!

DELRAY I already tried gettin' her on the blues station. They wanted money. I ain't got no money. And judgin' by the way you dress, I bet you ain't got no money either.

HUEY Ah hell, I ain't talkin' about some blues station only colored folks listen to! I'm gonna get her on a big- time station right in the center of the radio dial!

FELICIA   SO WHAT COULD BE THE HARM
IF I FALL FOR YOUR CHARM . . .

[HUEY *jumps onstage.*]

HUEY/FELICIA   JUST ONE LITTLE PECK
ON YOUR SWEET LITTLE NECK,
UNDER YOUR SPELL, UNDER YOUR COMMAND

HUEY   YOU GOT ME EATIN' OUTTA YOUR HAND!

HUEY/FELICIA   THERE ARE WORSE THINGS I COULD
DO

HUEY   AND I WANNA DO THEM ALL TO YOU—

HUEY   So, Miss Felicia, if I get you on the radio, maybe you and me could, ya know . . .

FELICIA   Maybe me and you could, I know, what?

HUEY   Maybe you and me could go out sometime or something.

[*Music and dancing stop. All look at* HUEY. *A beat.*]

FELICIA   You hear what this boy just said to me, Delray?

BOBBY   Your brother stepped in the back.

FELICIA   [*To* HUEY.] Well, lucky for you.

[*Music restarts.*]

You really gonna get me on the radio?

HUEY   I get on, you get on.

[HUEY *grabs the mike as they flirt and sing*]

AIN'T NOTHIN' BUT A KISS

FELICIA   AND THEN I'LL SHUT THE DOOR

HUEY   A SIMPLE LITTLE KISS

FELICIA   BUT NEXT TIME, YOU'LL GET MORE.
CAN YOU HANDLE THIS?

HUEY   I think so.

FELICIA   CAN YOU HANDLE THIS?

HUEY   Maybe not.

FELICIA   CAN YOU HANDLE THIS?
AIN'T NOTHIN' BUT A KISS!

SCENE 4

Streets of Memphis.

[HUEY *is out looking for a job.* STATION MANAGERS *appear.*]

"HELLO, MY NAME IS HUEY"

STATION MANAGER 1   WDBJ.

HUEY   HELLO, MY NAME IS HUEY, SIR!
I KNOW THIS MIGHT SOUND SCREWY, SIR!
BUT OH! I KNOW THE KIND OF MUSIC PEOPLE CRAVE!

[*We hear a door slam.*]

STATION MANAGER 2   WSAL.

HUEY   YOU SEE, I'M ON A MISSION, SIR,
TO BE IN A POSITION, SIR,
WHERE WE CAN MAKE THIS RED -HOT MUSIC
ALL THE RAVE!

[*We hear a door slam.*]

STATION MANAGER 3   WLXQ.

HUEY   BEFORE YOU SLAM THIS DOOR RIGHT HERE,
I'D LIKE TO MAKE MYSELF REAL CLEAR—

[*We hear a door slam.*]

SIMMONS WHDZ.

HUEY HELLO, MY NAME IS HUEY, SIR!
I KNOW THIS MIGHT SOUND SCREWY, SIR,
BUT OH! I KNOW THE TYPE OF MUSIC PEOPLE CRAVE!
YOU SEE, I'M ON A MISSION, SIR,
TO BE IN A POSITION, SIR,
WHERE WE CAN MAKE THIS RED -HOT MUSIC
ALL THE RAVE!

SIMMONS Son, I already got me a rhythm & blues DJ, Buck Wiley.

HUEY BUT WAIT! MY NAME IS HUEY, SIR!
AND IF YOU'D LISTEN TO ME, SIR,
YOU'D KNOW I KNOW THE KIND OF MUSIC FOLKS
WILL LOVE.

SIMMONS Wait a minute! Ain't you that boy that got fired from Collins Department Store for causin' that ruckus?

HUEY Yes, sir!

SIMMONS Tell you what, boy. I'm gonna do you a favor. Come inside and listen to ol' Buck Wiley and learn what a real disc jockey sounds like.

[*Lights up on the DJ booth.* BUCK WILEY, *an exceedingly white man, is at the microphone.* HUEY *crosses to listen in.*]

RADIO SINGERS [*Recorded.*] WHDZ—MEMPHIS.

WILEY Boy oh boy. Ladies and gents, this is Buck Wiley, your host of "Boppin' with the Blues"—playing you the bop bop boppinest music in Memphis. And now a special treat, a little song that's the favorite ditty of the wife and I whenever we want to cuddle up, drink some soda pop, and perhaps kiss. Here's Miss Patti Page . . .

[*He puts on a record.* BOBBY *enters, sweeping up.*]

"LITTLE OL' DOGGIE NAMED DOUGIE"

PATTI PAGE [*offstage.*] I'VE GOT ME A LITTLE OL' DOGGIE

BOBBY [*Riffing on the song.*] DOGGIE—

PATTI PAGE [*offstage.*] HIS NAME IS DOUGIE

BOBBY DOGGIE NAMED DOUGIE

PATTI PAGE [*offstage.*] ARF, ARF

HUEY Hey, hey! It's Huey from the club!

BOBBY Huey, what you doin' here?

HUEY Say, I didn't know you could sing like that

BOBBY Oh no, no, I was just, uh . . .

HUEY   So tell me somethin'. I thought this program was called "Boppin' with the Blues."

BOBBY   That's why I go to Delray's in the nighttime —to try and forget what this man's playin' in the daytime.

WILEY   Okay, folks, and now a hot, hot hit from Mr. Roy Rogers—

[ROY ROGERS *clippity- clop music plays.* WILEY *enters from his DJ booth, leaving the door open.*]

WILEY   And who are you?

HUEY   Oh, I'm a pal of ol' Bobby here.

[WILEY *looks at them suspiciously.*]

WILEY   [*To* BOBBY, *snapping his fingers.*] Boy, get me a Coca-Cola.

[WILEY *exits. As soon as he's gone,* BOBBY *finger -snaps back at him, then goes to get him a soda. Left alone,* HUEY *contemplates the tantalizingly open DJ booth. Suddenly,* HUEY *rushes into the DJ booth,, locks the door, and lunges for the microphone.* BOBBY *returns and rushes to him.*]

BOBBY   Hey, hey! No, no!

HUEY   [*Overlapping with* BOBBY.] Folks, this here's Huey

Calhoun and the police just came and arrested ol' Buck Wiley 'cause his show sure wasn't boppin' but it sure as heck was giving me the blues! Okay, folks, if you like the sweet sound of my sweet voice and you wanna hear some real music, call in as soon as you can!

[SIMMONS *rushes in, closely followed by* WILEY, *zipping his fly.*]

SIMMONS   What the hell is goin' on here?

WILEY   Hey! Hey!

[*Overlapping* HUEY.]

SIMMONS   Boy, you open that door, open that door!

[*As* SIMMONS *and* WILEY *frantically try to get into the booth...*]

HUEY   See, 'cause right now there are aliens—evil, ugly aliens—conspirin' to take me away from you! And remember, the name's Huey. That's right, rhymes with "Whooey!" Now let's get rhythm and bluey!

SIMMONS   Find the keys! Find the damn keys!

[HUEY *puts on a record.*]

"EVERYBODY WANTS TO BE BLACK ON SATURDAY NIGHT"

[*Lights up on an African American* SINGING TRIO.]

TRIO   EVERYBODY! EVERYBODY!
EVERYBODY WANTS TO BE BLACK ON SATURDAY
NIGHT!

BOBBY   All right!

TRIO   EVERYBODY! EVERYBODY!
EVERYBODY WANTS TO JUMP BACK
AND FEEL THEIR SPIRIT TAKE FLIGHT!
EVERYBODY WANTS TO BE BLACK!
EVERYBODY WANTS TO JUMP BACK!
EVERYBODY WANTS TO BE BLACK ON A SATURDAY
NIGHT!

[SIMMONS *and* WILEY *have gotten into the booth and they push* HUEY *aside.* WILEY *stops the record and gets on the air.*]

WILEY   Ladies and gentlemen, we are so sorry 'bout that crazy interruption. Now, let's get back to Roy.

[WILEY *puts on the* ROY ROGERS *music.*]

SIMMONS   Boy, you goin' straight to jail!

[*Phone rings.*]

HUEY Wait! Maybe that's a listener calling in their support.

SIMMONS Boy, none of my listeners are gonna support race music!

[*Music starts.*]

WILEY [*Answering it.*] WHDZ. How may I help you?

[*Spot up on* WHITE TEENAGE GIRL.]

"THAT'S NOT POSSIBLE"

WHITE TEENAGE GIRL WHAT YOU BOYS DOIN'?
GIMME MORE OF THAT HUEY!
PUT THAT HUEY ON,
GIMME MORE AND MORE!

BUCK WILEY ABSOLUTELY NOT, THAT'S NOT POSSIBLE.

[*Another phone rings.* BOBBY *answers it.*

BOBBY WHDZ—

[*A spot on* WHITE TEENAGE GIRL 2.]

WHITE TEENAGE GIRL 2 PUT THAT BOY, HUEY, PUT HIM ON!
I DANCED WITH THE DEVIL
WHEN HE PLAYED THAT SONG.

BOBBY   ABSOLUTELY NOT, THAT'S NOT POSSIBLE!

[*Phones continue to ring.*]

SIMMONS   WHAT THE HELL IS GOIN' ON IN THERE?

[*A spot on* TWO WHITE TEENAGE BOYS.]

TWO WHITE TEENAGE BOYS   PUT THAT HUEY ON
BEFORE MY PARENTS COME BACK!
HE PLAYS THE KIND OF MUSIC
MAKES ME FEEL LIKE I'M BLACK!

BUCK WILEY   ABSOLUTELY NOT, THAT'S NOT
POSSIBLE!

BOBBY   ABSOLUTELY NOT, THAT'S NOT POSSIBLE!

TEENAGE BOYS & GIRLS	**BOBBY**
NEVER HEARD NO MUSIC	ABSOLUTELY NOT,
LIKE THAT BEFORE!	NO, NO, NOT POSSIBLE
NEVER HEARD NO MUSIC	ABSOLUTELY NOT,
LIKE THAT BEFORE!	THAT'S NOT POSSIBLE
NEVER HEARD NO MUSIC	ABSOLUTELY NOT,
LIKE THAT BEFORE!	NO, NO, NOT POSSIBLE!
	NO, NO, NO, NO ...

BOBBY   [*Getting carried away.*] NO, NO, NO, NO, NO, NO,
NO, NO, NO, NO, NO—NO, NO, NO, NO, NO, NO, NO,
NO, NOT POSSIBLE, NO, NO, NO, NO, NO . . .

[BOBBY *stops, realizing the others are staring at him.*]

Sorry, no.

[BOBBY *quickly hangs up.* TEENAGERS *disappear.*]

HUEY   Sir, just gimme a chance and I'll get you more listeners than you ever had!

WILEY   Mr. Simmons, they only play that music on colored stations! And no God- fearing person listens to it!

SIMMONS   Then why are my damn phones ringin' like this?! All right, boy, I'm givin' you a two- week tryout.

WILEY   What?!

HUEY   How much it pay?

SIMMONS   Nothin'!

HUEY   I'll take it!

SIMMONS   And if the ratings don't go to shit and we don't all get killed, I'll hire ya!

WILEY   But sir, this is a white station!

SIMMONS   Well, he's white!

WILEY   Folks ain't gonna think so. Not when he's playin' race music!

SIMMONS   Boy, get on the air and tell 'em you're white!

HUEY   [*On the microphone.*] Hello, I'm white.

SIMMONS   Not like that! Just tell 'em—tell 'em what high school you went to!

HUEY   [*Back on the microphone.*] Folks, this is Huey Calhoun, who almost made it all the way through to the ninth grade at South Side High! Hockadoo!

[HUEY *puts the record back on as the* SINGING TRIO *reappears.* WILEY *and* SIMMONS *exit.*]

TRIO   EVERYBODY, EVERYBODY,
EVERYBODY WANTS TO BE BLACK
ON SATURDAY NIGHT!

[WHITE TEENAGE GIRL *appears, dancing with the radio.*]

EVERYBODY! EVERYBODY!
EVERYBODY WANTS TO JUMP BACK
AND FEEL THEIR SPIRIT TAKE FLIGHT. . .

EVERYBODY WANTS TO BE BLACK
EVERYBODY WANTS TO JUMP BACK

EVERYBODY WANTS TO BE BLACK
ON A SATURDAY NIGHT

[*Dance break.* WHITE TEENAGERS, *listening to their radios, join in.*]

EVERYBODY! EVERYBODY!
EVERYBODY WANTS TO BE BLACK
ON A SATURDAY NIGHT!

[MOTHER *sees her* DAUGHTER *dancing and singing.*]

MOTHER   [*Calling off.*] Do you hear what your daughter's listening to?!

DAUGHTER   [*Along with trio.*] EVERYBODY WANTS TO BE BLACK!

WHITE MOTHER   Do you hear it?!

DAUGHTER   [*Along with* TRIO.] EVERYBODY WANTS TO JUMP BACK!

[WHITE FATHER *enters.*]

WHITE MOTHER   Do something!

DAUGHTER   [*Along with* TRIO.]EVERYBODY WANTS TO BE BLACK ON SATURDAY . . .

[WHITE FATHER *slaps her. The music and the dancing abruptly stop.*]

SCENE 5

The Calhoun home. Later that week. Early Sunday morning.

[*A shack of a place.* HUEY *enters, finishing up a beer.* GLADYS, *in a dingy waitress uniform, sits.*]

HUEY   Mornin', Mama. What you doin' up? You work the night shift again?

GLADYS   A letter come for you, Huey.

HUEY   Oh, Mr. Simmons says I been gettin' lots of letters down at the station. You hear my program last night?

GLADYS   Can't put your program on at the diner. Good Christians come there.

HUEY   Why do good Christians always annoy me'?

GLADYS   Before you rattle on with your blasphemy, I'd like to read the letter. Could you hand it to me?

HUEY   Well, sure. Where is it?

GLADYS   On the floor. Tied to that brick.

[*A beat.*]

HUEY This don't mean nothin', Mama—

GLADYS I come home and turn on the lights and it come crashin' through the window like they was waitin' for me—

HUEY It don't mean nothin'!

GLADYS Huey, I want you to quit that radio!

HUEY It's just folks lettin' off steam.

GLADYS There is a brick on my floor!

HUEY Mama, listen I think I'm maybe finally good at something. Did you ever expect me to be good at something?

GLADYS No.

HUEY Yeah, well, this music   I think it might actually take me somewhere, somewhere better than this.

GLADYS Now you sound like your daddy. The man never even once left Memphis.

HUEY But, Mama, I met this girl.

GLADYS A girl?

HUEY Yeah, a nice girl and she's um . . .

GLADYS She's what?

HUEY Well, she's uh . . . Oh, Mama, you shoulda heard my program! I had on the good Reverend Calvin Hobson of First Baptist. And I says, now Reverend, how many white folks usually come by to hear your fantastical gospel choir?

[*Lights up on* REVEREND CALVIN HOBSON, *on the radio.*]

REVEREND HOBSON Uh, just you.

HUEY What?! Well, we gotta invite some white folks then!

REVEREND HOBSON I guess you can invite 'em, but trust me, they ain't gonna come.

HUEY All right, kids, now you listen to me and you listen good if you wanna hear some of the best music on God's good earth, go down and hear the good folks at First Baptist!

GLADYS You sent innocent white children down to a colored church?

HUEY Well, none have of 'em showed up or nothin' yet, but, Mama, this music, it's like my callin'.

GLADYS Your calling is playing race music for white folks?

[*Lights up on the* CHURCH CHOIR. REVEREND HOBSON *presides.*]

"MAKE ME STRONGER"

CHOIR/FELICIA   PICK ME UP. LIFT ME HIGHER.
GIVE ME STRENGTH I NEVER HAD
FOR I CAN'T BE WEAK TOO MUCH LONGER.
OH, LORD, LORD, LORD, MAKE ME STRONGER.

[*Split focus*—HUEY & MAMA *at home and the* CHOIR *at church.*]

HUEY   Kids been pickin' on me my whole life, so I ain't gonna be scared of no damn bullies throwin' bricks!

OH, MAMA, LISTEN TO ME.
THEY'RE TOO BLIND AND THEY JUST CAN'T SEE!
I'M BUYING YOU A HOME.
I SWEAR RIGHT NOW.
I SWEAR RIGHT HERE,
I'M GONNA MAKE THIS POVERTY DISAPPEAR!
I'M GONNA MAKE THIS POVERTY DISAPPEAR!

CHOIR   PICK ME UP
LIFT ME HIGHER
GIVE ME STRENGTH
I NEVER HAD

GLADYS   ALL MY LIFE I DONE WHAT'S PROPER

AND HERE WE ARE STILL POOR AS DIRT.
OH, I JUST CAN'T TAKE THIS TOO MUCH LONGER.
OH, LORD, LORD, LORD, MAKE ME STRONGER!
OH, LORD, LORD, MAKE ME STRONGER!

[HUEY *goes to the church and joins in the* CHOIR. *Lights remain on* GLADYS *in her home.*]

CHOIR   FEEL HIS LOVE

FELICIA   FEEL HIS LOVE

CHOIR   FEEL HIS POWER

FELICIA   FEEL HIS POWER

CHOIR   MOVE A MOUNTAIN

FELICIA   MOVE A MOUNTAIN

CHOIR   CHANGE THE WORLD

FELICIA   GONNA CHANGE THE WORLD

CHOIR   FOR I CAN'T BE WEAK

FELICIA   I CAN'T BE WEAK

FELICIA/CHOIR   TOO MUCH LONGER.
OH, LORD, LORD, LORD, MAKE ME STRONGER.

OH, LORD, LORD, LORD, MAKE ME STRONGER.

[THE WHITE TEENAGE GIRL *enters the church. All stop and look at her. A beat.*]

TEENAGE GIRL   That boy said it'd be all right if I came by.

REVEREND HOBSON   What boy?

TEENAGE GIRL   You know—the one on the radio. The funny-talkin' one.

HUEY   I hear he's real handsome, too.

FELICIA   Well, I'll be . . .

[FELICIA *takes the girl's hand.*]

[*A cappella.*]

PICK ME UP

TEENAGE GIRL   PICK ME UP

FELICIA   LIFT ME HIGHER

TEENAGE GIRL   LIFT ME HIGHER

GLADYS   GIVE ME STRENGTH

HUEY GIVE ME STRENGTH

GLADYS I NEVER HAD

[*Music in.*]

CHOIR NEVER HAD!

TEENAGE GIRL/FELICIA/CHOIR FOR I CAN'T BE
WEAK TOO MUCH LONGER.
OH, LORD, LORD, LORD, MAKE ME STRONGER.

CHOIR FEEL HIS LOVE

[GLADYS *cleans up the broken glass as the church celebration
continues.*]

GLADYS [*Responds throughout.*] FEEL HIS LOVE

CHOIR FEEL HIS POWER

GLADYS FEEL HIS POWER

CHOIR MOVE A MOUNTAIN

GLADYS MOVE A MOUNTAIN

CHOIR CHANGE THE WORLD

GLADYS CHANGE THE WORLD

CHOIR FOR I CAN'T BE WEAK

GLADYS I CAN'T BE WEAK

CHOIR TOO MUCH LONGER

GLADYS TOO MUCH LONGER

CHOIR OH LORD, LORD, LORD
MAKE ME STRONGER
OH LORD, LORD, LORD
MAKE ME STRONGER

[GLADYS *exits.*]

FELICIA HE MAKES ME STRONGER

CHOIR MAKES ME STRONGER

FELICIA HE MAKES ME STRONGER

CHOIR MAKES ME STRONGER

FELICIA WHEN I AM WEAK

CHOIR MAKES ME STRONGER

FELICIA HE MAKES ME STRONG

CHOIR MAKES ME STRONGER

FELICIA   HE LIFTS ME UP

CHOIR   MAKES ME STRONGER

FELICIA   WHEN I AM DOWN

CHOIR   MAKES ME STRONGER

FELICIA   HE PUTS MY FEET, MY FEET

CHOIR   MAKES ME STRONGER

FELICIA   ON SOLID GROUND

CHOIR   MAKES ME STRONGER

CHOIR with FELICIA   [*Riffs.*] MAKES ME STRONGER/
MAKES ME STRONGER.
MAKES ME STRONGER/MAKES ME STRONGER.
MAKES ME STRONGER/MAKES ME STRONGER.
MAKES ME STRONGER/MAKES ME STRONGER.
OH—LORD, LORD, LORD, MAKE ME STRONGER.
OH—LORD, LORD, LORD.

FELICIA   MAKE ME/MAKE ME

CHOIR   STRONGER

SCENE 6

[HUEY *in the DJ booth.* SIMMONS *and* BOBBY *look on.* GATOR *sits off to the side. Music underscores.*]

HUEY [*Into mike.*] Hockadoo! This is Huey Calhoun, your new host of "Boppin' with the Blues," the number-one program in Memphis!

SIMMONS What's he talkin' about, number-one program? He's only been on the air four days.

HUEY [*Into mike.*] Comin' at you on radio station, W, uh, W, uh, now what is the name of this radio station again?

SIMMONS WHDZ!

HUEY What?

SIMMONS WHDZ!

HUEY What?

SIMMONS WHDZ!

HUEY [*Into mike.*] WRNB!

SIMMONS What?!

HUEY [*Into mike.*]Yes, sir, WRNB!

SIMMONS   He can't change our call letters like that!

BOBBY   I think he just did, sir.

HUEY   [*Into mike.*] See, Mama, your heathen son is makin' good on the radio! Hockadoo!

SIMMONS   And what the hell does "hock…uh?"

BOBBY   Hockadoo.

SIMMONS   Yeah, what the hell does that mean? Is that dirty?

[HUEY *enters from the radio booth.*]

HUEY   Show's goin' great, ain't it?

SIMMONS   Calhoun, this "Hockadoo!" What the hell's it mean?

HUEY   Don't know, sir. Just felt like saying it and out it came!

SIMMONS   You shouldn't say words you don't know the meaning of. People think they're dirty! And remember, I'm just trying you out. [*Referring to* GATOR.]

And what's this boy doin' here?

HUEY   I don't rightly know. Gator don't talk none. He lives behind the bar in Delray's. First time I ever seen him out.

SIMMONS   Calhoun, even your friends annoy me. All right, now here's today's commercial. Read it at least three times in the next hour.

HUEY   You want me to read it?

SIMMONS   Exactly as it says! You can read, can't you?

HUEY   Uh, yes, sir!

SIMMONS   Then read it exactly as it says! That's the way our sponsor wrote it, so that's the way they want it. I'll be listenin'!

   [SIMMONS *exits.*]

HUEY   Oh, shit.

BOBBY   Huey, you don't know how to read?

HUEY   Hey Bobby, could you read this to me?

BOBBY   No, I can't. Mr. Simmons would have my hide if he found out.

HUEY   Bobby, if I don't get this right, he's gonna fire me and bring back ol' Buck Wiley and you gonna be listenin' to "Little Ol' Doggie Named Dougie" for the rest of your life!

BOBBY   [*Taking the script.*] Okay.

[*Reading.*]

I'd like to announce that Dryer's Grocery Store is having a sale on my favorite beer, Dupont Beer. M, m, m, m, m.

HUEY   M, m, m, m, m?

BOBBY   Oh, they must mean, "Mm, mmm."

HUEY   "Mm, mmm." Got it.

BOBBY   [*Reading.*] Whenever I'm thirsty, I have Dupont Beer. Mm, mmm. It's a good beer for drinking.

HUEY   Good for drinkin'? What the hell else you gonna do with it?

BOBBY   Well that's what it says.

   [*Reading.*]

So get to Dryer's Grocery and buy Dupont Beer. The best beer in Memphis. Mmmm.

HUEY   Thanks kindly!

   [HUEY *rushes into the booth.*]

   [*Into the mike.*]

Folks, I got me a message from the good folks down at Dryer's Grocery. Let's see now: Seems ol' Dryer's is having a big sale on Dupont Beer. "Mm, mmm," spelled m m m m m . . .

BOBBY No, no—

HUEY Now, um, it's my favorite beer—yes, sir—and it's, uh, it's, uh . . .

[*He looks over at* BOBBY *in a panic.*]

BOBBY Good for drinkin'!

HUEY What?!

BOBBY Good for drinkin'!

HUEY Oh, it's good for drinkin', which seems pretty darn obvious to me . . . Aw heck, folks, listen up, this beer is so good, it's not only good for drinking, but you can put it in your gas tank and it'll make your car run!

BOBBY What?

HUEY That's right! So when you're sitting around snugglin' up with your wife or someone else's wife, well, you just take a big ol' swig of Dupont and it'll turn you into a beer -swillin' love machine. So you drink it with meals, between meals, for breakfast, for lunch, all day, and all night. And if for some strange reason you don't drink beer, well, you rub it all over your head and watch all your hair grow back! Folks, this beer's so good, your naggin' wife will shut up, your kids will stop screaming, and your dog will stop lickin' his privates! Yes, sir, this is Huey Calhoun, who spends his days talkin' on the radio and his nights gettin' loaded on Dupont Beer! So you run right down to Dryer's and tell ol' Frank Dryer, "Hockadoo!"

[HUEY *puts on a record.*]

BOBBY   It was nice knowin' ya.

[SIMMONS *rushes in.*]

SIMMONS   Calhoun!

HUEY   Before you fire me, sir, I just thought if it sounded more like the way I speak, then maybe folks'll be thinkin', well, if ol' Huey likes it, then I like it, too . . .

BOBBY   [*Answering the phone.*]WRNB . . .

SIMMONS   Hey!

BOBBY   WHDZ!

SIMMONS   Boy, you are out of control!

BOBBY   [*On phone.*]Uh, sir?

SIMMONS   What?!

BOBBY   It's Mr. Dryer!

SIMMONS   [*Takes phone.*]Hello—

[*Lights up on* FRANK DRYER, *on the phone in his store.*]

FRANK DRYER   Hank, would you tell me what in hell is going on down at your station? A bunch a' kids just ran in like a mess of hogs and they been buyin' beer and yellin', "Hockadoo!"

MR. SIMMONS   I'm sorry, Frank. I got this lunatic deejay, who I'm firing right now!

FRANK DRYER   Firing him? I ain't never sold this much beer this fast! I want that boy doing my ads every day!

MR. SIMMONS   What?

FRANK DRYER And by the way, "Hockadoo"? Is that dirty?

SCENE 7

The Calhoun home. A month later.

[HUEY *is dancing in his own private world.*]

HUEY   OH, THE SPONSORS LOVE ME,
YES THEY DO, THEY LOVE ME.
I'M SELLIN' LOTS OF BEER, NOW

SELLIN' LOTS OF BEER.
OH, THIS GIRL, SHE DIGS ME,
YES SHE DOES, SHE DIGS ME . . .

[FELICIA *enters and catches* HUEY *smack in the middle of a ridiculous dance move.* HUEY *stops. A beat.*]

FELICIA   Am I interruptin' something?

HUEY   Uh, well, no, I was just, well, I don't know what the hell I was just doin'.

FELICIA   I was knockin' but . . . anyway, I suppose I shouldn't be in this neighborhood.

HUEY   I suppose you shouldn't. Anyone bother you?

FELICIA   A coupla boys made a coupla remarks. Nothin' I ain't heard before. Oh, just don't tell my brother I came! He'd kill me if he knew.

HUEY   I thought he sorta liked me.

FELICIA   Uh, no. So—I always thought white folks homes were nicer than black folks homes.

HUEY   Can I offer you some lemonade or somethin'?

FELICIA   Actually, I been listenin' to your radio program, and, as a sort of congratulations, I brought you a present.

[*She takes a can from her purse.*]

HUEY   Well, I'll be a can of Reynold's Beer. How'd you know what I wanted most?

FELICIA   Well, I was gonna get you some Dupont Beer, but they said 'cause of you, they always sold out.

HUEY   Well, tell you the truth, Dupont Beer tastes kinda like pee. So you really come all the way here just to gimme a can of beer?

FELICIA   It's just you haven't been to the club in three nights and, well, I wanted to make sure you was all right is all.

HUEY   Oh. [*Realizes.*] But you said you been listenin' to me on the radio –

FELICIA   Yeah.

HUEY   So you knew I was all right, so . . . I guess you must be here 'cause—

FELICIA   'Cause why?

HUEY   'Cause you missed me.

[*He laughs, a little.*]

FELICIA   Now don't be gettin' all high on yourself—

HUEY [*Still laughs.*]You missed me .

FELICIA I will be going now—

HUEY No, wait, no, I, uh, I missed you, too.

FELICIA Oh, yeah?

HUEY Oh, yeah.

FELICIA Huey, I been thinkin'—you know how you always promisin' that you'll play my record as soon as I can afford to make one. Well, I ain't no fool, I know that when a man promises me something, he wants something in return.

HUEY Well, that'd be right.

FELICIA [*She steps back.*] Oh. Right.

HUEY And know what I want? To play your sweet, sweet voice for all my radio listeners.

FELICIA And?

HUEY And—I'd like to drink this beer.

FELICIA That all?

HUEY Play your sweet voice and drink this beer, yep, that's it.

FELICIA   Nothin' more? Really?

HUEY   Well, really I do want somethin' more. But not in return for gettin' you on the radio. I want more 'cause, I was hopin' maybe you'd maybe want more. Maybe. Or somethin'. I don't know. I'm enjoyin' this beer.

[*He nervously takes a sip.*]

FELICIA   I'm gonna venture a guess and say that you haven't kissed a lot of girls.

HUEY   A couple, maybe. I'd like to do more of that, though . . . You kiss a lot of boys?

FELICIA   A few.

HUEY   Ever kiss a white one?

FELICIA   No, can't say I ever kissed a cracker boy. Wouldn't be wise of me, would it?

HUEY   Be downright foolish.

FELICIA   Dangerous.

HUEY   Oh, yeah.

FELICIA   Huey, I got a surprise.

HUEY   Another can of beer?

[*She takes a single record from her bag.*]

What's that?

FELICIA   "Someday"—the very first record of Felicia Farrell!

HUEY   What?

FELICIA   We finally saved up enough money and Delray got some boys from the club and we recorded it yesterday!

HUEY   Why didn't you tell me you was doin' this!

FELICIA   Delray didn't want you stoppin' by and interferin'.

HUEY   I think your brother really likes me more than he's lettin' on.

FELICIA   No, he doesn't. Oh, Huey, this record means the whole wide world to me, so you really gonna keep your promise?

HUEY   You're gonna come to the radio station tomorrow and I'm gonna go on the air and say—All right, boys and girls, I got me the very first record of Miss Felicia Farrell! Why, her singin' is so hot, it's gonna melt everythin' in your icebox! It's gonna make your grandma faint, your grandpa lose his teeth, and it's—

[GLADYS *enters. At first* HUEY *and* FELICIA *don't notice her.*]

gonna make your little baby stand up in his diapers and shout, "I believe! I believe in the power of. . .

[*Notices* GLADYS *and stops.*]

Mama. Hi.

GLADYS   Who is this?

HUEY   Mama, this is, uh, well, this is the girl I was telling you about.

GLADYS   Have you lost your mind?!

HUEY   Mama—

GLADYS   Playin' their music is one thing—

HUEY   Now, Mama, she's a singer, a fine singer—

GLADYS   This is a good Christian household.

HUEY   She's a Christian.

GLADYS   She ain't nothin' but a colored girl!

HUEY   Mama!

FELICIA   I should go—

HUEY   Mama, look, she made this record! I'm gonna play it on the radio tomor—

[GLADYS *slaps the record out of* HUEY's *hands, breaking it in two. a beat.* FELICIA *picks up the two halves of the record.*]

FELICIA   I'm sorry to have bothered you, ma'am.

[FELICIA *rushes out of the house.*]

HUEY   Mama, how could you do that?

GLADYS   What in the hell is wrong with you?

[HUEY *rushes out.*]

Huey!

SCENE 8

An alley outside HUEY's *home.*

HUEY   Miss Felicia!

FELICIA   I let myself believe you! I actually let myself believe you for a moment.

HUEY   At least come to the radio station tomorrow.

FELICIA With two halves of a record?!

HUEY We'll go to the recording studio, have 'em make another copy!

FELICIA There is no other copy! This is all we could afford.

HUEY So come to the station, we'll figure somethin' out!

FELICIA Delray's right, I been actin' like a fool.

HUEY Well, don't you understand—this is your big chance!

FELICIA No!

"COLORED WOMAN"

SOME GOT CHANCES,
SOME GOT CHOICES,
SOME GOT FREEDOM
IN THESE STATES.

COLORED WOMEN
GOT FEW CHANCES,
GOT FEW CHOICES
ON OUR PLATES.

MAMA TOLD ME
THERE ARE LIMITS
FOR DARK -SKINNED GIRLS

STUCK IN THIS LIGHT -SKINNED WORLD.

ONCE IN A WHILE
I LOSE MYSELF IN DREAMS.
A SILLY GIRL
FULL OF SILLY SCHEMES.

NOW ALONG COMES A MAN
WHOSE SKIN IS WHITE AND PALE.
A SHINY FOOL
FULL OF SHINY TALES.

HE SAYS HE'LL MAKE
THE PEOPLE HEAR ME.
HE'LL FORCE THIS WORLD
TO FIN'LY SEE ME.

IS HE A LIE
LIKE EV'RY OTHER MAN—
OR LORD
COULD HE SOMEHOW

HUEY   COULD HE SOMEHOW

FELICIA   COULD HE SOMEHOW HELP TO FREE ME

All right, Huey, I'll see you at your radio station tomorrow.

HUEY   You swear it?

FELICIA   [*She touches his cheek.*] Huey Calhoun, if you want me there, I will be there.

HUEY   I want you there.

[HUEY *exits.*]

MAMA TOLD ME
NOT TO DREAM BIG,
BUT MAMA LIVED HER LIFE RUNNING SCARED.
I AM STRONGER
AND I'LL FIGHT LONGER!
I'LL DO WHAT MAMA NEVER EVEN DARED!

COLORED WOMAN
WITH FEW CHANCES,
HAS TO DO WHAT
SHE MUST DO!

I WILL MAKE MY
COLORED DREAMS COME TRUE!
FOR THIS IS ONE COLORED WOMAN
WHO WILL COLOR HER LIFE—
HER WAY!

SCENE 9

[*Lights up on* HUEY *in the DJ booth. In the studio,* GATOR *hangs out as* BOBBY *cleans and* MR. SIMMONS *listens.*]

HUEY Hockadoo! This is "Boppin' with the Blues" with your fantastical radio pal, Huey, celebrating two months of bein' on the air! And, Mama, Mr. Simmons is payin' me now and everything! Hockadoo!

SIMMONS Say, Bobby . . .

BOBBY Sir?

SIMMONS I ever tell you I have a son?

BOBBY Uh, no, sir.

SIMMONS Really? I never mentioned that?

BOBBY You never mention nothin' to me, sir.

SIMMONS Well, he's fifteen, sixteen, something like that. And he thinks I'm the most useless man on the planet. His contempt for me is astounding. That is, until he heard about Calhoun—and for the first time ever, he started listenin' to my station. He started likin' my station. And once in a while now, the little son of a bitch actually talks to me.

[BOBBY *crosses away.* HUEY *enters from the booth.*]

HUEY Hey, Gator, any sign of her?

[BOBBY *shakes his head "no."*]

SIMMONS Calhoun, I gotta talk to you—

HUEY The ratings come in yet?

SIMMONS Not yet but . . .

HUEY I bet ol' Huey is number one now!

SIMMONS Calhoun, how you gonna be number one? Last month, you was number five. Shows don't jump up in the ratings like that.

HUEY But everywhere I go, everyone says how much they love ol' Huey!

SIMMONS Not everybody. Folks get all crazy when things start changin' too fast—

[FELICIA *enters. A beat.*]

Can I help you?

HUEY Oh, this is Miss Felicia Farrell, Mr. Simmons.

FELICIA Hello, sir.

HUEY I wanted her to come see the station.

SIMMONS What for?

HUEY She's a singer. She made a fantastical record.

SIMMONS Calhoun, it's fantastic.

HUEY Why, thank ya.

SIMMONS No, the word, it's fantastic, not fantastical. I don't always know what's goin' on in that unexceptional brain of yours, Calhoun, but I do got limits.

[SIMMONS *exits.*]

FELICIA You should've told the man I was coming.

HUEY Ah, he has no control over who I put on my program.

FELICIA How'm I gonna be on your program? Your mama broke my record.

HUEY Right. So you're gonna have to sing live.

FELICIA Live? I ain't singin' live on no radio.

[GATOR *places a microphone in front of her.*]

But what'm I gonna do for music?

HUEY Vernon! James! Elroy!

[*Three musicians enter.*]

MUSICIAN Hey, Felicia.

FELICIA Well, I ain't singin' on the radio without my back up singers.

HUEY Selma! Laverne! Bessie!

[*They enter and happily wave at* FELICIA.]

[*Into mike.*]

I'm back, folks, and I'd like y'all to meet the fantastical Miss Felicia Farrell. Miss Felicia just signed a big -time record contract with the newest big- time record label in the business, Delray Records.

FELICIA What?

HUEY That's right and—whoa, hold on! Take a look at where Felicia Farrell is right now!

FELICIA Where am I?

HUEY Right smack in the center of the radio dial. This, folks, is what I mean by the music of my soul.

[*A beat.*]

Look, if you don't wanna do this—

FELICIA Mr. Calhoun

HUEY   Yeah?

FELICIA   Hold my purse.

[*She steps up to the mike.*]

"SOMEDAY"

One-two-one-two-three-four.

FELICIA/BACK UPS   SOMEDAY, I'M GONNA DO YOU
WRONG
SOMEDAY I'LL LEAVE YOU . . .

FELICIA   BLUE

BACK UPS   LEAVE YOU BLUE

HUEY   Hit it, boys!

[*Music in.*]

FELICIA   SOMEDAY I'M GONNA STEAL YOUR HEART.
SOMEDAY I'LL RIP IT RIGHT IN TWO.
BUT SOMEDAY JUST AIN'T HERE YET
AND I'M STILL STUCK ON YOU,
SO LET'S JUST SAY WE GOT TODAY
AND DO WHAT LOVERS DO.

FELICIA	BACK UPS
	AH OOH
SOME NIGHT I'M GONNA	
HURT YA BAD	AH OOH
SOME NIGHT I'LL CAUSE	
YOU PAIN	AH OOH

FELICIA   SOME NIGHT I'M GONNA LEAVE YA DRY 'N'

FELICIA and BACK UPS   CRYIN' IN THE RAIN

FELICIA	BACK UPS
	AH OOH
BUT SOME NIGHT JUST	
AIN'T HERE YET	AH OOH
AND BOY YOU'RE LOOKIN'	
GOOD	AH OOH
SO LET'S PRETEND	
TONIGHT WON'T END AND	

FELICIA and BACK UPS   ACT LIKE LOVERS SHOULD

[HUEY *grabs the microphone.*]

HUEY Now, boys, don't that pretty voice make your heart go "oh," your lips go "wow" and other parts of ya just go crazy? That's what it do to me, so maybe this fine woman will give me a big ol' kiss—

FELICIA and BACK UPS SOMEDAY—

FELICIA I'M GONNA DO YOU WRONG
SOMEDAY I'LL LEAVE YOU BLUE

BACK UPS LEAVE YOU BLUE

FELICIA and BACK UPS SOMEDAY—

FELICIA I'M GONNA STEAL YOUR HEART
SOMEDAY I'LL RIP IT RIGHT IN TWO

BACK UPS I'LL RIP IT RIGHT IN

FELICIA BUT SOMEDAY JUST AIN'T HERE YET
AND I'M STILL STUCK ON YOU

[DELRAY *enters and watches.*]

FELICIA and BACK UPS SO LET'S JUST SAY WE GOT TODAY,
SO LET'S JUST SAY WE GOT TODAY,
SO LET'S JUST SAY WE GOT TODAY
AND DO WHAT LOVERS DO!

[*Music buttons.*]

FELICIA Delray, did you hear? Did you hear?!

DELRAY Yeah, I heard, baby girl—especially the part when he said he was gonna kiss you.

FELICIA I should go, Huey—

DELRAY Gator, walk her home.

FELICIA Huey, you will visit the club soon.

HUEY Sure will.

[*She and* GATOR *exit.*]

DELRAY What world you livin' in, boy? You want to get us all killed?

HUEY You know what, Del? I think you're jealous!

DELRAY What?

HUEY I say I'm gonna put your sister on the radio and, bam, I put her on the radio. I said I was gonna take this music and . . .

DELRAY But you ain't lived this music! You ain't made this music! It ain't your music to take!

HUEY So what then? You gonna keep your sister singin' in your crappy little club—

DELRAY Now hold on, you redneck son of a bitch!

[*Music starts.*]

"SHE'S MY SISTER"

DELRAY NOW I DIDN'T MEAN TO CALL YOU
A REDNECK SON OFA BITCH.
THOUGH YOU ARE A REDNECK SON OF A BITCH.
I KNOW YOU DIDN'T MEAN
TO CALL MY CLUB A CRAPPY LITTLE CLUB.
THOUGH I GUESS IT IS A CRAPPY LITTLE CLUB.
MY PARENTS DIED YOUNG.
THEY DIED POOR.
THEY LEFT ME WITH MY SISTER,
NOT MUCH MORE.

SHE HAD THIS VOICE
LIKE NONE I KNEW
SO I OPENED UP MY CLUB
WHAT ELSE COULD I DO?

FOR MY SISTER

HUEY She means somethin' to me, too.

DELRAY MY LITTLE SISTER

HUEY   And I think I mean somethin' to her!

DELRAY   SHE SANG HER SONG AND THE CUSTOMERS CAME

HUEY   I CAME FROM NOTHIN'

DELRAY   WE MADE SOME MONEY
AND I MADE ME A NAME

HUEY   I'LL MAKE HER SOMETHIN'

DELRAY   YOU'RE STEALIN' THIS MUSIC

HUEY   THAT AIN'T FOR YOU TO SAY

DELRAY   HEY, I DON'T BLAME YA, BROTHER,
IT'S THE AMERICAN WAY

HUEY   NO, NO, THERE'S SOMETHING YOU JUST
DON'T UNDERSTAND

DELRAY   YEAH, I UNDERSTAND YOU'RE A
DANGEROUS MAN

HUEY   OH I LOVE YOUR SISTER, REALLY I DO

DELRAY   DON'T EVER LET ME HEAR THOSE WORDS
COME OUT OF YOU!
NOT HERE IN MEMPHIS—

DELRAY Here's somethin' I never showed you—

[DELRAY *reveals a serious scar on his shoulder.*]

HUEY Jesus. How'd you ?

DELRAY I took a sip from "whites only" drinking fountain.

HUEY Well, why in the hell did you do that?!

DELRAY 'Cause I was fourteen. And I was thirsty.

DELRAY THE DANGER IS DEEP
THAT YOU WANNA PUT HER IN
I DON'T CARE ABOUT YOU
BUT SHE'S MY SISTER

I'M A GOD- FEARING MAN,
A CHRISTIAN THROUGH AND THROUGH—
BUT YOU CAN BET I'LL PROTECT MY BABY SISTER
OH, OH, OH, SHE'S MY ONE AND ONLY FLESH AND
BLOOD.
BE CAREFUL WITH THE ONE I LOVE.
SHE'S MY SISTER.

[DELRAY *exits.* SIMMONS *enters.*]

SIMMONS Calhoun! You know I'm a man of business. I make
my decisions on what's best for my pocketbook.

HUEY Are you firing me?!

SIMMONS Calhoun, I don't like this music. I don't understand it. But the ratings just come in. You got the number-one show in Memphis. I'm gonna make me a shit-load of money. You're gettin' a three-year contract! Hocka fuckin' doo!

[SIMMONS *exits.* HUEY *stands, somewhat stunned, by his sudden change of fortune.* FELICIA *enters.*]

FELICIA Hey. I hope you don't mind me coming back, but I owe you somethin', don't I?

"AIN'T NOTHIN' BUT A KISS" REPRISE

TAKE A TASTE OF THIS
AIN'T NOTHIN' BUT A . . .

[*She goes to him, and they kiss.*]

SCENE 10

A street in Memphis. Several months later.

HUEY Mama!

[GLADYS *enters.*]

Mama, would you keep up with me!

GLADYS   Huey, why'd you drag me to this neighborhood?

HUEY   Mama, I gotta show you something—

GLADYS   Don't keep avoidin' me, Huey! You been avoidin' me for months and I know where you been—sneakin' around with that colored girl! Well, it's gotta stop!

HUEY   Aw, Mama, would you stop your naggin' and listen to me—your good for nothin' son is actually makin' somethin' of himself!

"RADIO"

HUEY   HOW MANY TIMES DID I HEAR IT?
HOW MANY TIMES DID THEY TRY? TO SOMEHOW
BREAK MY SPIRIT, TO SOMEHOW MAKE ME DIE—

[*As he sings, projections appear featuring photographs and the following headlines:*

HUEY CALHOUN PRESENTS FIRST ALL RHYTHM & BLUES CONCERT

WHITE TEENAGERS FLOCK TO ALL NEGRO CONCERTS

12 ARRESTED AT CALHOUN'S R&B CAVALCADE

CITY COUNCIL THREATENS TO BAN CALHOUN CAVALCADE CONCERTS

HUEY "HUEY, YOU'RE ODD, CRAZY, AND SLOW.
NOT MUCH TO LOOK AT."
WELL, MAYBE THAT'S SO.
THEY TRIED SO HARD
TO DRAG ME DOWN LOW.
THEY DIDN'T COUNT ON
COUNT ON THE RADIO! THE RADIO!

[*Newspaper photographer enters with* MR. SIMMONS.]

PHOTOGRAPHER Hey, Huey!

[HUEY *smiles and the* PHOTOGRAPHER *flashes his picture.*
PHOTOGRAPHER *exits.*]

HUEY I KNEW IT COULD TEACH
I KNEW IT COULD PREACH—
I KNEW IT COULD REACH
ACROSS THE AIR!

[*Two* AFRICAN AMERICAN GIRLS *enter.* HUEY *signs an
autograph book.*]

I KNEW IT COULD SELL
I KNEW IT COULD YELL
I KNEW IT COULD TELL
THE TRUTH OUT THERE!

GLADYS That girl touched me.

HUEY NOT BAD FOR A BACKWARD HICK!
NOT BAD FOR A COUNTRY KID!

GLADYS Take me home, Huey!

HUEY NOT A BAD LITTLE OL' TRICK
TO DO ALL THAT I DID!

GLADYS I ain't listenin' to no more boastin.' Boastin' is a sin.

HUEY Mama, you see that house up there.

GLADYS What about it?!

HUEY I bought it for you.

GLADYS What? You ain't serious?!

HUEY And Mama, I'm sorry for bein' so boastful.

GLADYS Oh, a little boastin' never hurt nobody!

[GLADYS *rushes into the house. She stops for a moment.*]

HUEY Hockadoo.

GLADYS Oh, Huey—

[*She exits.* HUEY *takes a moment and lets it all soak in. A beat.*]

HUEY   Hockadoo! This is Huey Calhoun bringin' you the best rhythm and blues in America—right smack in the center of your radio dial!

[*Two groups of* TEENAGERS *come out to play, segregating themselves along racial lines.*]

TEENAGERS   WE LOVE WHEN IT SINGS
WE LOVE WHEN IT SWINGS

HUEY   I LOVE WHEN IT BRINGS
MY SOUL TO YOU—

TEENAGERS   WE LOVE WHEN IT HOPS
WE LOVE WHEN IT BOPS

HUEY   THE RIDE NEVER STOPS—
JUST FEEL IT COME THROUGH!
SO TURN THE VOLUME UP NOW!
LET THE MUSIC HAVE ITS SAY!
AIN'T NO USE IN HOLDIN' BACK.
THE RHYTHM'S GONNA GET YOU,
THE RHYTHM'S GONNA GET YOU,
THE RHYTHM'S GONNA GET YOU ANYWAY!

[*Dance break. As the* TEENAGERS *play, they desegregate themselves.*]

TEENAGERS   WE LOVE WHEN IT SINGS—WE LOVE
WHEN IT SWINGS—

HUEY   I LOVE WHEN IT BRINGS MY SOUL TO YOU—

TEENAGERS   WE USE IT TO JIVE. WE USE IT THRIVE

HUEY   AND I CAME ALIVE—

TEENAGERS   ON THE/ON THE RADIO!

HUEY   THE RADIO!

SCENE 11

Beale Street.

> [FELICIA *waits as a* TEENAGE GIRL *passes by carrying a radio. The radio is playing* FELICIA*'s recording of "Someday." The girl sings along as* FELICIA *watches.*]

TEENAGE GIRL   SOMEDAY I'M GONNA DO YOU WRONG.
SOMEDAY I'LL LEAVE YOU BLUE.

> [*The* GIRL *giggles and rushes off as* HUEY, *wearing a very flashy jacket, rushes on.*]

HUEY   Hey, baby—

FELICIA   You just hear that? They were playin' "Someday" on the radio—

HUEY 'Cause it's a great record, baby—

FELICIA But it never made it much outside of Memphis. And they're still playin' it—

HUEY They love you in Memphis. They understand you in Memphis. Just like I love and understand you. And I'm in Memphis.

FELICIA You really smooth.

[*He moves in to kiss her, but she steps away.*]

HUEY C'mon now

FELICIA It's still a little light out, Huey. By the way, what are you wearin'?

HUEY Oh, I wanted to spruce up real special for the first party of Delray Records—what you think?

FELICIA I think you need a woman besides your mama to start pickin' out your clothes. C'mon now, Delray's gonna have our hides if we're late.

HUEY Wait, I wanna give you somethin'.

FELICIA What?

HUEY Somethin'. Nothin'. This.

[*He holds out a ring box. She looks at it. A beat.*]

Well, take it and open it. It's all paid up, ain't even on layaway.

[*A beat.*]

See, I guess I'm tired of sneakin' around with you, like—like you was a bad thing. These two years with you—they been the best ever. So I guess what I'm tryin' to say is —

[*He gets down on one knee.*] Would you be the woman to pick out my clothes for the rest of my life? Marry me.

FELICIA Get up, Huey, now. Now.

[*He does.*]

You really talkin' crazy. How we gonna get married? There are laws.

HUEY So we go on a trip up north, get hitched, come back . . .

FELICIA And then do what? Live together in secret?

HUEY See, I been thinkin'. I don't know how secret we'd need to be. I'm the most popular fellah in Memphis—I think folks would come to accept us.

FELICIA I'm glad Delray wasn't here to hear this. And you know someday I wanna have a family, a baby. How we gonna have a baby?

HUEY The usual way—

FELICIA We gotta get goin'.

HUEY All right, answer me this. Pretend we don't got none of them crazy laws in Tennessee—pretend two grown adults can marry who they like. Then would you marry me?

FELICIA Huey, c'mon—

HUEY Stop walkin' and answer me! Would you marry me? Would ya?

[FELICIA *stops for a moment, thinks.*]

FELICIA I—I would. Yes. I would.

HUEY Well, that's good, that's good. Why don't you take this ring and keep it somewhere, 'cause I think maybe things are changin', maybe a little. You hear about that Negro lady in Alabama, the one who wouldn't give up her seat on that bus? Well, they got some boycotts goin' on down there or something and . . .

[FELICIA *suddenly throws caution to the wind and kisses* HUEY. *Two* WHITE MEN *enter.*]

WHITE MAN 1   Well, if it ain't Huey Calhoun Whooey.

[FELICIA *and* HUEY *quickly break away from their kiss.*]

HUEY   Sorry, boys, we're in a bit of hurry . . .

[*Two more* WHITE MEN *enter to surround them. Suddenly one of the men raises a baseball bat. A trumpet screams. One of the men holds down* HUEY *as the others beat up* FELICIA.]

WHITE MAN 2   Hockadoo!

[*Scene shifts to Delray's, where a party is going on.*]

DELRAY   All right, a few years ago now, this white boy, this crazy cracker—walked into my club. And he said he was gonna get my sister on the radio. And I didn't trust him, ya know, 'cause, well—he was white.

[PARTYGOERS *laugh.* HUEY *carries in* FELICIA, *who is bloody and beat up and barely conscious.*]

HUEY   Someone help—

DELRAY   Oh, Jesus!

HUEY   They hurt her bad.

CLUBGOER   I'll call an ambulance!

HUEY They came at us with bats . . .

CLUBGOER Make sure it's a colored ambulance!

CLUBGOER Call a white one for Huey!

HUEY No, I'm okay, just get one for her . . .

DELRAY Oh my God, oh my God . . .

HUEY I tried to stop them, but they held me down.

DELRAY Speak to me, baby girl—

HUEY I tried to stop them . . .

BOBBY Be quiet now, Huey—

DELRAY Speak to me, baby girl— [*Yells to* HUEY.] I knew it! I told you this would happen!

BOBBY Calm down, Del—

DELRAY This is your fault! Your damn fault!

[DELRAY *steps toward* HUEY. *The others try to pull him off.*]

BOBBY Del, no! No!

DELRAY I told you! I told you!

[FELICIA *comes to, a bit.*]

FELICIA   Delray?

[DELRAY *goes back to her.*]

DELRAY   Oh, baby girl, you're gonna be all right, you're gonna be all right, you hear? Help is on the way.

FELICIA   How's Huey?

HUEY   Felicia, I'm right here.

DELRAY   Stay away from her— [*To* FELICIA.] Hush now, just hush.

CLUBGOER   The ambulance is on the way!

FELICIA   Huey . . .

HUEY   Felicia—

DELRAY   You son of a bitch! I told you this was gonna happen!

BOBBY   Shut up, Del!

[DELRAY *slams a chair down.*]

DELRAY   I'm gonna kill you! I swear I'm gonna—

[*He advances on* HUEY.]

I'm gonna kill you!

[GATOR *steps in between* HUEY *and* DELRAY.]

GATOR   Stop!

[*All stop and look at* GATOR.]

"SAY A PRAYER"

GATOR   SAY A PRAYER
THAT CHANGE IS COMIN'.
SAY A PRAYER
THAT HOPE IS ROUND THE BEND
AND IF YOU PRAY
THAT CHANGE IS COMIN', OH, JESUS—
THEN MAY WHAT YOU PRAY
COME TRUE
AMEN

CLUBGOER   Ambulance is here!

[DELRAY *carries* FELICIA *up the stairs to the ambulance.*]

CLUBGOERS   SAY A PRAYER

GATOR   THAT CHANGE IS COMIN'.

CLUBGOERS SAY A PRAYER

BOBBY THAT HOPE IS ROUND THE BEND.

CLUBGOERS AND IF YOU PRAY THAT CHANGE IS COMIN', OH—

GATOR OH, JESUS—THEN MAY WHAT YOU PRAY

CLUBGOERS PRAY

HUEY MAY WHAT YOU PRAY—

GATOR PRAY

ALL MAY WHAT YOU PRAY COME TRUE. AMEN!

End of Act 1

ACT 2

SCENE 1

Several months later.

[HUEY *stands in front of a test pattern.*]

GATOR   Hey, Huey, you sure you know what you're doin' here?

HUEY   I think that's my secret, I never know what the hell I'm doin', I just do it.

GATOR   Hockadoo.

STAGE MANAGER   All right, and in five—four—three . . .

HUEY   Can you believe it, Memphis?! They gave me my own TV show?!

[HUEY's *afternoon TV show comes alive.* AFRICAN

AMERICAN TEENAGERS *dance up a storm.*]

"CRAZY LITTLE HUEY"

HUEY   CRAZY LITTLE HUEY WAS SOME CRAZY
LITTLE FOOL!
CRAZY LITTLE HUEY LIKED TO BREAK EV'RY RULE!
CRAZY LITTLE HUEY HEARD WHAT NO ONE SAID!
THAT CRAZY WHITE BOY WAS CRAZY OUT OF HIS
HEAD!
HE LOVED THAT BLACK MUSIC
THOUGH HE'S WHITE AS A GHOST!

DANCERS   WHITE AS A GHOST!

HUEY   HE PLAYED IT ANYWAY, NOW HE'S A TV HOST!

DANCERS   TV HOST!

HUEY and DANCERS   'N' HE'S GOT MORE SUCCESS
THAN FOLKS EVER DREAMED—

HUEY   THAT CRAZY WHITE BOY AIN'T CRAZY AS HE
ONCE SEEMED!

[*Focus on* SIMMONS *taking to* GLADYS *off to the side.*]

SIMMONS   Mrs. Calhoun, I can't believe I let your son talk me
into an all-Negro program.

Felicia (Montego Glover) takes the stage in "Underground."

Delray (J. Bernard Calloway) and Felicia celebrate the joys of singing "Underground."

Huey extols "The Music of My Soul."

ABOVE: Felicia finds her strength in "Colored Woman."

LEFT: Felicia brings Huey to his knees at the end of "Ain't Nothin' But a Kiss."

Huey and the Teenagers at the end of "Radio."

A white and a black teenager double Dutch in "Radio."

Huey encourages Felicia to sing "Someday" live on the radio.

Teenagers dance up a storm in "Radio."

Huey watches the teenagers dance in "Radio."

Teenagers celebrate their new music in "Radio."

ABOVE: Bobby (James Monroe Iglehart) leads the African-American dancers in "Crazy Little Huey."

LEFT: Huey and Felicia about to steal a dangerous kiss on the streets of Memphis.

Felicia lays down her latest recording, "Love Will Stand When All Else Falls."

Gladys Calhoun (Cass Morgan) leads Gator (Derrick Baskin), Bobby (James Monroe Iglehart), and Delray (J. Bernard Calloway) in "Change Don't Come Easy."

The company performs the finale, "Steal Your Rock 'n' Roll."

GLADYS   Has he been earnin' you a whole mess of money?

SIMMONS   Yeah.

GLADYS   Then shut up.

HUEY   THIS CRAZY WHITE BOY AIN'T CRAZY AS HE ONCE SEEMED!

Show 'em kids!

   [*Dance break.*]

DANCERS   WE TALKIN' NON STOP BE BOP DO WOP A, BABY SLIPSLOPA FLIP FLOPA TIP TOP, BABY

HUEY   NAME IS HUEY!

DANCERS   HUEY!

HUEY   GIMME HUEY!

DANCERS   HUEY!

HUEY   SCREWY HUEY!

DANCERS   HUEY!

HUEY and DANCERS   CRAZY LITTLE HUEY IS ON YOUR TV!

[*Music buttons.*]

BOBBY   Hey, kids, it's time for Huey Calhoun's new after-school television program! And he's letting me be on it!

[*A siren goes off.*]

HUEY   You know what that means? It's time for the Gator dance!

[GATOR *and* THE DANCERS *break into an alligator dance.* HUEY *crosses to* FELICIA, *standing off to the side.* GLADYS *watches nearby.*]

HUEY   Baby, how come you ain't dressed yet?

FELICIA   I thought I could go on, but I just can't.

HUEY   But it's my very first show! And you're my surprise guest singer!

FELICIA   No, I just don't want people talkin' more—

HUEY   No one's talkin' . . .

FELICIA   Ever since that night, people been whisperin' we're together. And what're folks gonna say if they see me on your program?

GLADYS   That's good sense, Huey.

HUEY Mama, could you stand over there!?

[GLADYS *crosses away.*]

C'mon, just sing one song for me—

FELICIA You don't need me. Your program, it's lookin' kinda good in a stupid sort of way. I'm real proud of ya, sugar.

HUEY Hey, you do know what I wish more than anything, right?

FELICIA To be a big TV star.

HUEY No. I wish that what they done to you, they done to me instead. You do know that, don't you?

FELICIA I know that, sugar, I really do.

[GATOR *dance buttons.*]

BOBBY Uh, Huey.

HUEY Promise me you'll come on soon, okay?!

[HUEY *steps back in front of the camera.*]

We got a great show for you today, kids. Hockadoo!

DANCERS Hockadoo!

HUEY Now I know what you're all thinkin'—"Huey, you so ugly, how'd you ever get on the TV?" Well, Mr. Simmons—went and bought himself this here station—put a camera on the old man, boys—

[*The camera goes in on the startled* SIMMONS.]

So I says to him, "Hey, let's put on some rock 'n' roll"—and he says, "Boy, that's crazy, no one's ever put rock 'n' roll on TV before"— so I say, "Good, then no one knows what the heck's gonna happen!" And then he says, "Huey, you ugly but I love you," and he gives me a big ol' kiss on the lips!

SIMMONS That last part is not true! That is not true!

HUEY Here's the interferin' woman who gave birth to me—my mama! So I want y'all to say hi to the old lady right now!

DANCERS Hi, old lady!

GLADYS Huey, what do you think you're doing? I just come to watch.

HUEY Well, you're on the TV now, Mama.

GLADYS I am?

HUEY Say hello to Memphis, Mama!

GLADYS Hi, Memphis!

HUEY Attention, all you elderly gentlemen out there! This here fine-looking woman has already buried one husband and she's lookin' to bury another.

GLADYS That's right, I am. I am!

HUEY Oh, this here's our announcer, ol' Bobby Dupree!

DANCERS Hi, ol' Bobby Dupree!

HUEY I met Bobby when he was moppin' floors at WRNB. But turns out what he always wanted to do was sing songs for the people, but they ain't never given him a chance. Ain't that right, Bobby?

BOBBY I guess.

HUEY And, Bobby, you know how I said we was gonna have a surprise singer on the show today?

BOBBY Uh- huh.

HUEY Well, that singer's you!

BOBBY What?!

HUEY Surprise!

BOBBY No, no . . .

HUEY   But, Bobby, you sound so nice when you sing in the men's washroom.

BOBBY   But this ain't the men's washroom.

HUEY   Well, just pretend it is. From the top, Vernon!

[*Music starts.* BOBBY *freezes.*]

Men's room, Bobby.

[*Music starts again.*]

"BIG LOVE"

BOBBY   SOME PEOPLE SAY I'M JUST A FOOL,
A MAN WITH NOTHIN' TO SHOW

HUEY   Ain't he pretty, girls?

BOBBY   THEY SAY I GOT THE CHARM OF A MULE,
BUT THERE'S SOMETHING THEM PEOPLE DON'T
KNOW

HUEY   Now smile, Bobby—

BOBBY   IF THEY COULD JUST SEE DEEP INSIDE,
THEY'D SEE THAT MY HEART CAN SING.
I GOT MY SOUL AND I, I GOT MY PRIDE
AND I GOT ME ONE OTHER THING—

[*And* BOBBY *suddenly comes alive.*]

TWO—THREE —FOUR!

OPEN YOUR EYES
I GOT A SURPRISE!
WE'LL BE ROCKIN' 'N' A-ROLLIN'
TILL WE SEE THE SUNRISE!
LIKE ROMEO,
I'LL TAKE YOU PLACES YOU NEVER GO!
CALL ME BIG DADDY!
'CAUSE BIG DADDY'S GOT BIG LOVE!

ALL THE PRETTY BOYS TRY TO GET THEIR KICKS!
BUT I'M THE CITY BOY WHO GETS ALL THE CHICKS!
I THINK YOU'LL DIG
THE PART OF ME THAT'S BIG!
CALL ME BIG DADDY
'CAUSE BIG DADDY'S GOT BIG LOVE!

Watch this, Mama!

[*Dance break.* BOBBY *dances like a man half his age and size.*]

CALL ME BIG DADDY.
YOU'LL FLIP YOUR WIG FOR BIG DADDY!
TAKE A SWIG OF BIG DADDY
'CAUSE BIG DADDY'S GOT BIG LOVE!

SCENE 2

HUEY's *living room.*

[*He lives in a fairly nice apartment now.* FELICIA *is studying sheet music. As she softly sings, she is finishing getting dressed.*]

FELICIA   THE SUN IS SINKIN' AND TIME'S GOT ME THINKIN' . . .

HUEY   [*offstage.*] I'm number one, baby! Woo!

FELICIA   AS WE GROW OLD . . .

[HUEY *enters. He's also finishing getting dressed—buckling his pants, buttoning his shirt.*]

HUEY   Number one on radio and when the ratings come in, I bet I'm gonna be number one on TV, too. Me, who can't even spell TV. Hey, what's that you singin' there?

FELICIA   New song I been writin' some lyrics for, gonna lay it down today.

HUEY   Today? How come I didn't know about this?

FELICIA   Just came up. And you been so busy with your program, didn't want to bother you is all.

HUEY   Since when is you layin' down a song botherin' me?

[*Kisses her on the neck.*]

Mm, glad you came for a visit, baby—

FELICIA Hey, sugar, what if we could do more than visit?

HUEY So be honest—am I the best lover you ever had?

FELICIA Yeah, okay. But what if we could do more than visit? What if we could get out of Memphis?

HUEY Whaddya mean?

FELICIA I mean—what if we could get up north, to New York.

HUEY Ain't nothin' worth visitin' in New York, baby. Wait— always wanted to see that Coney Island. That in New York?

FELICIA Don't rightly know. But what if we could stay?

HUEY In Coney Island?

FELICIA What if Delray got someone from New York to come down and hear me, someone who could really help.

HUEY Don't get your hopes up, baby, your brother's been tryin' to do that for years.

FELICIA But if Delray could get someone here—

HUEY   Besides, the man who's gonna make you famous is me! All you gotta do is come on my TV show!

FELICIA   But up north—

HUEY   And you know what else—I'm takin' you to that Coney Island!

FELICIA   But up north—

HUEY   Just as soon as we figure out where the hell it is.

FELICIA   Up north, I wouldn't have to be sneakin' into your apartment like this. We could be together, we could be happy . . .

HUEY   It's like you talkin' Chinese, baby. We are happy, we are together

FELICIA   We could be safe up north.

[A beat.]

HUEY   Baby, I got this plan! See, you gonna come on the Cavalcade and folks gonna take one look at ya and they gonna love you the way they love me. How could they not, huh? We ain't gonna have to leave Memphis 'cause we gonna be Memphis. This is our home, baby. And what them fellahs done to you, if I could only go back and . . .

[A beat.]

Hey, this song you was singin'—

[*Music starts.*]

You come on my TV show and sing it for me and Huey's gonna make everything okay

[*She begins to hum.*]

I ain't ever lettin' anyone hurt you ever again, I swear that.

"LOVE WILL STAND WHEN ALL ELSE FALLS"

FELICIA   THE SUN IS SINKIN'
AND TIME'S GOT ME THINKIN'.
AS WE GROW OLD, WILL OUR LOVE STAY STRONG,
OR WILL IT DISAPPEAR?

HUEY   You the music of my soul, baby.

[*She nods. He exits.*]

FELICIA   TOMORROW'S UNKNOWN,
BUT TODAY IS OUR OWN.
SO TAKE MY HAND, HOLD ON WITH NO FEAR . . .

[*Transition to scene 3.*]

SCENE 3

[A recording studio. BACK UP SINGERS *flank* FELICIA. *In the recording booth,* DELRAY *and* GORDON GRANT, *a white record executive, observe.]*

FELICIA and BACK UP SINGERS 'CAUSE BABY, 'CAUSE BABY, 'CAUSE BABY—

FELICIA I'M HERE.
I WILL

FELICIA and BACK UP SINGERS SEE YOU THROUGH.

FELICIA I'LL BE—

FELICIA and BACK UP SINGERS THERE FOR YOU.
WE WILL ENDURE
WHAT LIFE HAS IN STORE.

FELICIA HAVE FAITH AND BELIEVE

FELICIA and BACK UP SINGERS LIKE THE AIR THAT YOU BREATHE,
LOVE WILL STAND WHEN ALL ELSE FALLS.
LOVE WILL STAND WHEN ALL ELSE FALLS.

FELICIA WHOA, I'VE BEEN PUT THROUGH HELL
MORE THAN I CAN TELL

FELICIA and BACK UP SINGERS   NOW I FINALLY SEE!

FELICIA
WHOA, THERE'S ONE WAY TO LIVE
BE KIND—

FELICIA and BACK UP SINGERS AND FORGIVE.
I HAVE THE POWER IN ME!

BACK UP SINGER   I HAVE POWER IN ME!

[*Instrumental solo.*]

FELICIA   FOLLOW WHERE I LEAD,
I'LL MEET EV'RY NEED.
WE WILL ENDURE

FELICIA and BACK UP SINGERS   WHAT LIFE HAS IN
STORE.

FELICIA   HAVE FAITH AND BELIEVE
LIKE THE

FELICIA and BACK UP SINGERS   AIR THAT YOU
BREATHE

[HUEY *enters, stands off to the side.*]

LOVE WILL STAND WHEN ALL ELSE . . .
FOLLOW WHERE I LEAD

I'LL MEET EV'RY NEED.
WE WILL ENDURE
WHAT LIFE HAS IN STORE.

FELICIA   HAVE FAITH AND BELIEVE
LIKE THE AIR

FELICIA and BACK UP SINGERS   THAT YOU BREATHE,
LOVE WILL STAND WHEN ALL ELSE FALLS.

FELICIA   LOVE WILL STAND WHEN ALL ELSE FALLS.
OOOO OOO OOOO . . .

[HUEY *crosses and claps.*]

HUEY   Whooey.

FELICIA   Huey, what you doin' here?

HUEY   Well, I was at the station and Bobby was wonderin' why I wasn't at your recording session. And I said she's just layin' down a new song, and he said, yeah, for a big-time record producer. From up north!

FELICIA   Baby, it just came together a couple of days ago, I'll explain later .

[DELRAY *and* GORDON *enter from the control booth.*]

DELRAY   Huey—

HUEY   Hey there, Del, so what's goin' on here?

FELICIA   I hope you enjoyed the song, sir.

HUEY   Hell, who wouldn't enjoy it! She's the best singer in Memphis and I discovered her!

DELRAY   What?

HUEY   So who you?

GORDON   Gordon Grant, RCA Records.

HUEY   Huey Calhoun. Number-one TV and radio man in Memphis!

GORDON   That's very nice.

[*Crosses to* FELICIA.]

So, ma'am, I was telling your brother that you sing Negro music, but the kind of Negro music that I think white folks might like. Have you ever sung this new music, this rock 'n' roll?

FELICIA   Sure. All rock 'n' roll is, is Negro blues sped up.

GORDON   Well, that's not exactly true.

DELRAY   Actually, sir—

DELRAY and FELICIA   It is.

HUEY   This man thinks good white folks like you and me stole this music! You believe that?!

GORDON   Well, I don't really care if anyone stole it or not, 'cause the fact is—kids are buyin' it. So, Miss Farrell, if it's all right with you, I'd like you to come to New York for a bit, and if things work out, I'd like to try and get you on every radio station in the country.

FELICIA   What?

HUEY   No –

DELRAY   Are you serious?

GORDON   I wouldn't waste my time if I wasn't. Is there some-place in town where we might be allowed to dine together this evening?

FELICIA   I know this one chicken joint.

GORDON   Fine, I'll pick you both up here at seven. We can get better acquainted then.

HUEY   Wait a minute now, I discovered this young lady! And they didn't even tell me they was auditioning for you today! And me and her are . . .

FELICIA   Huey, please!

GORDON   If you don't mind—you and her are what?

[*A beat.*]

Look, I understand that artists sometimes operate on a different moral plane than the rest of us. Lena Horne is married to a Jewish fellow, but they are the epitome of discretion.

HUEY   Yeah, well, what does "epitome" mean?

FELICIA   It means if people find out about us, the record company will drop my contract.

GORDON   That's right.

HUEY   Felicia, we gotta talk. I don't think this New York is such a good idea—

GORDON   Would it be a better idea, Mr. Calhoun, if you came with her?

HUEY   What?

GORDON   Well, the networks are trying to figure out how to put rock 'n' roll on TV.

HUEY   Well, I figured that out already!

GORDON Okay then, so how about I send someone down to see your television show. No promises, but with a little polish, you well may be what they're looking for.

HUEY What? Really?

GORDON You'd be seen coast to coast. I'll set something up. Miss Farrell, you really are special. And, Mr. Calhoun, you really are unique. TV might just love you. See you at seven.

[*He exits.*]

HUEY That guy for real?

DELRAY He's for real and you almost blew it!

[*To* FELICIA.]

This man cannot come to New York with us!

HUEY Hey, don't go tellin' me where I can and can't go!

FELICIA Now the two of you have to shut your mouths—

DELRAY We almost lost her 'cause of you! She can't have children 'cause of you!

HUEY Now hold on—

DELRAY They will laugh at you in New York!

HUEY   What?

FELICIA   I said shut your mouths! Now you listen to me, Delray—we were wrong, we should've told Huey that we were doin' this today.

"STAND UP"

YOU SEE THAT FOOL . . .
JUST STANDIN' THERE
HE'S AS FOOL AS A FOOL CAN BE

HUEY   Hey!

FELICIA   BUT THAT CRAZY FOOL
IS THE MAN I LOVE,
SO THAT FOOL IS COMIN' WITH ME—

DELRAY   Felicia.

FELICIA   ALL OF THESE YEARS YOU'VE LOOKED
AFTER ME
AND I THANK YOU FROM DEEP DOWN IN MY SOUL.
BUT TODAY IS THE DAY
I'VE WORKED FOR ALL OF MY LIFE,
SO STEP ASIDE, YEAH, I'M TAKIN' CONTROL.
UNROLL THE RED CARPET
AND UNCORK THE CHAMPAGNE,
WE'RE FLYIN' TO NEW YORK ON A BIG OL'
AEROPLANE.

IT'S TIME WE STAND UP—
C'MON—

DELRAY   STAND UP.

FELICIA   That's better—

DELRAY   MAKE NEW YORK HEAR OUR SONG.

FELICIA   DON'T YOU KNOW IT'S TIME TO STAND UP.

Now you.

HUEY   STAND UP!

HUEY and FELICIA   TIME TO PROVE THAT WE
BELONG.

DELRAY   I'LL GET RESPECT
I NEVER HAD,
BE A MUSIC -MAKIN' VIP!

HUEY   I'LL BE THE FIRST
TO PLAY THAT UNDERGROUND SOUND.
I'LL ROCK 'N' ROLL THEIR BLACK 'N' WHITE TV!

FELICIA   YOU'RE THE MAN I LOVE
 AND THE BROTHER I NEED—
BUT YOU BOTH BEEN GETTIN' ON MY NERVE.

DELRAY   SO WE GO UP NORTH.

HUEY   TO WHERE THE YANKEES LIVE.

FELICIA, HUEY, and DELRAY   AND LIVE THE LIFE THAT WE DESERVE!

[*Transition to* HUEY'S *TV show.* BOBBY *and the* DANCERS *are on air.*]

BOBBY   OL' BOBBY DUPREE
WAS JUST PUSHIN' A BROOM!
NOW I'M ON YOUR TV,
TEARIN' UP THE ROOM!
I MET ME A GIRL AND I MAKE HER GO—

BOBBY and ETHEL   WOW!

ETHEL   HE'S MY COOL CAT

BOBBY   AND SHE'S THE CAT'S MEOW!

[*Off to the side,* DELRAY *and* GATOR *watch.*]

DELRAY   So you know what your friend Huey's plannin' on doin' next? Puttin' up a speaker outside the studio.

GATOR   Why?

DELRAY   So bow legged white kids can dance along with us

GATOR   Huh. I sorta like that idea.

DELRAY   It ain't smart.

GATOR   I know, but I like it.

NOW IT'S TIME WE STAND UP! STAND UP!
MAKE 'EM ALL HEAR OUR SONG!

[DELRAY *exits.* GATOR *goes on camera and leads the* DANCERS.]

DON'T YOU KNOW IT'S TIME TO
STAND UP! STAND UP!

GATOR and DANCERS   STAND UP! STAND UP!

GATOR   GONNA PROVE THAT WE BELONG!

GATOR and DANCERS   WE TALKIN' NON STOP BE BOP
DO WUP A, BABY
SLIPSLOPA FLIP FLOPA TIP TUP, BABY

GATOR   TIME TO STAND UP!

DANCERS   TIME TO STAND UP! YEAH!

GATOR   TIME TO GET DOWN!

DANCERS   GET DOWN!

[*Transition to: Outside the studio. A loudspeaker has been set up, and* WHITE TEENAGERS *are dancing, shadowing the dance moves inside.* GLADYS *is smoking, watching.* HUEY *leads on* FELICIA.]

HUEY   [*Referring to the outside speaker.*] And here's my latest stroke of Calhoun genius

[*They watch the dancers.*]

GLADYS   Huey, them kids shouldn't be out here on the street dancin' like that.

HUEY   Mama, quit your worryin'.

[*To* FELICIA.]

How fantastical is it you about to make your Cavalcade debut!

FELICIA   I am sorry it's taken me so long, just had to feel ready.

DANCERS and TEENAGERS   WE TALKIN' NON STOP
BE BOP DO WUP A, BABY
SLIPSLOPA FLIP FLOPA TIP TUP, BABY
TIME TO GET DOWN! GET DOWN!
TIME TO GET DOWN! GET . . .

[*Two* WHITE MEN *enter. One rips the speaker off the wall. The other fires a gun into the air.*]

FELICIA   Oh!

[*The kids scatter.* HUEY *protects* FELICIA. *The men exit.* FE-LICIA *cowers.*]

HUEY   It's okay, baby, they gone now. You okay, Mama?

GLADYS   I'm fine, but you best take her outta here, Huey.

FELICIA   But I'm supposed to come on your show.

GLADYS   You go on some other time.

HUEY   She's right, baby

FELICIA   No. I'm tired of feelin' like this.

[*Focus on: the Cavalcade* DANCERS. HUEY *goes on camera.*]

HUEY   For the first time ever on your TV—Miss Felicia Farrell!

[FELICIA *emerges from the dancers.*]

FELICIA   [*Clap chorus.*] STAND UP IN THE NAME OF ROCK!

DANCERS   STAND UP!

FELICIA   GONNA ROLL YOU WITH MY SONG! CAN'T EVER LET THIS MUSIC STOP!

DANCERS   STAND UP!

FELICIA   THIS TRAIN IS ROLLIN' ON.

FELICIA	**DANCERS (2 GROUPS)**
DON'T YOU KNOW IT'S TIME	
	A: IT'S TIME TO STAND UP!
STAND UP!	
	B: STAND UP!
MAKE 'EM ALL HEAR OUR SONG	
IT'S OUR TIME TO STAND UP!	
	A: STAND UP!
	B: MAKE 'EM ALL HEAR OUR SONG!
PROVE THAT WE BELONG!	
	DANCERS
DON'T YOU KNOW IT'S TIME TO	STAND UP!
STAND UP!	
I SAID IT'S TIME TO STAND UP!	STAND UP!
DON'T YOU KNOW IT'S TIME TO	STAND UP!
STAND UP!	
	DANCERS
IT'S OUR TIME TO STAND UP!	STAND UP!
I SAID IT'S TIME TO STAND UP!	STAND UP!

DON'T YOU KNOW IT'S
TIME TO   STAND UP!
STAND UP!
STAND UP!

FELICIA   GONNA PROVE THAT WE BELONG!

SCENE 4

TV studio dressing room. A couple weeks later.

[SIMMONS, DELRAY, GLADYS, GATOR, *and* HUEY, *who is dressed garishly.*]

SIMMONS   Calhoun, now you gotta calm down and you gotta do what I say! The man from the network's gonna be here any minute!

HUEY   I ain't calmin' down and I ain't doin' what you say!

SIMMONS   I ain't lettin' you blow this, Calhoun! They promised me I could be one of the producers of your show!

HUEY   Well, ain't no one gonna watch my show if I listen to you. You see what he wants me to wear? A suit! Me, Huey Calhoun, in a suit! It's gonna scare the little children in TV land!

DELRAY   But it's your chance to go to New York.

SIMMONS   So you gotta look better than you do.

HUEY   But wouldn't they want to see what I'm really like?

GATOR   Uh-uh, no way, no, no, no, no way.

HUEY   Gator, I liked it better when you didn't talk none.

SIMMONS   You ain't the only rock 'n' roll show they're considerin.' There's that boy from Philadelphia, that Richard Clark. The network thinks he's very promising.

DELRAY   Listen, you can put on the suit or not. But my sister's going with or without you.

[BOBBY *enters.*]

BOBBY   The man from the network's here—

SIMMONS   You got five minutes to get dressed, Huey!

[SIMMONS *exits.*]

HUEY   But you know what I'm gonna look like if I put this on—an undertaker!

GLADYS   That's it, I heard enough. Huey, shut the hell up and do what they say.

HUEY   Mama, stay out of this.

GLADYS The hell I will. Look at you. You look like a Christmas tree with a drinking problem. And this is—this is your one decent chance to be with that girl of yours.

HUEY What?

GLADYS You heard me.

HUEY Mama, since when do you approve of . . . ?

GLADYS I don't approve. But you and that girl—

HUEY Her name's Felicia.

GLADYS You and that girl are gonna do what you wanna do anyway, right?

HUEY Right.

GLADYS Well, I don't like it.

[*Referring to* DELRAY.]

And he don't like it. But if you gotta be with her that bad—Memphis ain't no place for you.

DELRAY If I may add somethin'—

GLADYS Was I talkin' to you? No.

HUEY   Mama, This ain't like you.

GLADYS   Hell, I know.

[*Music in.*]

That's why last Sunday I went down to that colored church you always blabbin' on about. To pray on it.

HUEY   Mama, you stepped inside a colored . . .

"CHANGE DON'T COME EASY"

GLADYS   YEAH, I WENT TO THEIR CHURCH
AND HEARD THEM PEOPLE PRAY AND CHANT,
AND YOU WAS RIGHT 'BOUT ONE THING, HUEY–
COLORED FOLK SING LIKE WHITE PEOPLE CAN'T!

And that Reverend Hobson—I had no idea! Why, that man talked like he was dancin'.

HE TOLD US TO PRAY SOME,
HE TOLD US TO SWAY SOME,
HE TOLD US THE GOOD LORD MADE US EQUAL
INSIDE.
HE TOLD US WE WERE SINNERS,
HE TOLD US WE WERE WINNERS,
HE TOLD US TO CHANGE OR OUR SPIRITS WILL DIE.
BUT CHANGE DON'T COME EASY,
YOU GOTTA BELIEVE ME.

IT AIN'T GONNA HAPPEN OVERNIGHT.
CHANGE DON'T COME QUICKLY,
NO, NOT PARTIC'LY.
IT TAKES TIME TO MAKE ALL THE WRONGS RIGHT.
HE SAID CHANGE DON'T COME EASY.

[BOOBY, DELRAY, *and* GATOR *back her up.*]

TRIO NO, DON'T COME EASY

GLADYS CHANGE NEVER COMES EASY

TRIO NEVER COMES EASY

GLADYS I WAS TAUGHT TO HATE THEM,
WAS TAUGHT TO DENIGRATE THEM.
I WAS TAUGHT THEY'RE LESSER IN THE GOOD LORD'S
EYES.

TRIO OOH!

GLADYS CAN'T DRINK FROM THE SAME FOUNTAIN,
I'LL SCREAM IT FROM THE MOUNTAIN.

TRIO HEY!

GLADYS I'M THROUGH BUYIN' ALL THEIR
BLASPHEMOUS LIES!

GLADYS and TRIO BUT CHANGE DON'T COME EASY

GLADYS   YOU BETTER BELIEVE ME,
THAT IS SOMETHIN' THAT YOU CAN'T REFUTE

GLADYS and TRIO   CHANGE DON'T COME QUICKLY

GLADYS   NO, NOT PARTIC'LY,
SO GET IN THERE AND PUT ON THAT SUIT!
I SAID CHANGE DON'T COME EASY.

TRIO   LISTEN TO YOUR MAMA

GLADYS   CHANGE NEVER COMES EASY

TRIO   SO STOP WITH ALL THE DRAMA

GLADYS   Now put it on!

[HUEY *grabs the suit and exits. She turns toward* DELRAY.]

And now I'm talkin' to you.

MY BOY LOVES YOUR SISTER,
WE BOTH KNOW THAT, MISTER.
THIS AIN'T NO TEMPORARY PHASE.
'CAUSE MY BOY IS STUPID.
HE'S BEEN SHOT BY CUPID
SO WE GOTTA CHANGE OUR INTOLERANT WAYS.

THE REVEREND HELPED ME FIND MY WAY
TO CARRY ON AND PRAY

THAT THERE'S A BETTER DAY!
SO WON'T YOU COME JOIN ME!
YOU GOTTA COME JOIN ME!
JOIN ME AS I TESTIFY!

TRIO   YEAH!

GLADYS   WOO! GOTTA ELECTRIFY!

GATOR   ELECTRIFY!

GLADYS   GONNA MYSTIFY!

BOBBY   MYSTIFY!

GLADYS   WE GONNA GLORIFY!

GATOR and BOBBY   GLORIFY!

GLADYS   YOU KNOW I WANNA PRETTIFY!

DELRAY   PRETTIFY!

GLADYS   IT'S ALL ABOUT DO OR DIE!

TRIO   DO OR DIE!

GLADYS   COME ON, EVERYBODY—JUSTIFY!

TRIO   JUSTIFY!

GLADYS   HEAR MY BATTLE CRY!

TRIO   BATTLE CRY!

GLADYS   EASY AS APPLE PIE!

TRIO   APPLE PIE! OOH!

GLADYS   I GOTTA TESTIFY! ONE, TWO!

GLADYS and TRIO   CHANGE DON'T COME EASY!

SCENE 5

[*The TV studio—ten minutes into the show.* WAILIN' JOE *is wailin' up a storm and the dancers dance.*]

"SCRATCH MY ITCH" REPRISE

WAILIN' JOE   BABY, BABY, BABY
BABY, BABY, BABY
BABY, BABY, BABY,
YOU'RE GIVING ME A TWITCH
SO SCRATCH MY ITCH!

[HUEY *steps forward, now wearing a business suit.*]

HUEY   That was Wailin' Joe and this is Huey Calhoun.

GATOR   Your local undertaker.

HUEY   Okay, kids, time to sell ya some more junk you don't need.

GATOR   And comin' up soon . . .

HUEY   Felicia Farrel!

STAGE MANAGER   . . . and we are out!

[HUEY *crosses to* MARTIN, SIMMONS, DELRAY.]

SIMMONS   Huey, get over here, get over here! Say hello to Martin Holton, from the network.

HUEY   Hey there, Mr. TV Man, so what'd you think so far?

MARTIN   Well, I think you're a funny fellow, Mr. Calhoun.

HUEY   You mean "ha-ha I like you" funny or "ha- ha you're an idiot" funny?

MARTIN   To be honest, I'm not quite sure. But you're definitely different than anyone I've ever seen on television. And that is good.

SIMMONS   How good?

MARTIN   Well, good enough that your boy here just may give that Dick Clark a run for his money.

SIMMONS Hockadoo!

DANCERS Hockadoo!

MARTIN Of course, there's much to discuss, the timing, the format, the necessary changes.

SIMMONS That all sounds fine, Martin!

HUEY Yeah, if you're talkin' about me changin' out of this here suit, it's really, really itchy.

MARTIN Actually, I quite like the suit. I was talkin' about your dancers.

HUEY My dancers?

SIMMONS Everyone, could you give us a moment, please—

[*The* DANCERS *step back away from them.*]

MARTIN Perhaps we should discuss this following the program?

HUEY No, say what's on your mind. What don't you like 'bout my dancers? They got the best feet in Memphis!

MARTIN Mr. Calhoun, I'm talking a national broadcast. So naturally the network would insist on white dancers. Why surely you must've assumed this?

HUEY   Why would I assume my rhythm and blues show won't have none of the folks who make rhythm and blues?

MARTIN   I'm sorry, but we just can't get sponsors with a Negro show. Even Nat King Cole can't get sponsors, and he's the only Negro on his program.

SIMMONS   Martin, I think you're right , let's discuss this afterwards. The boy will listen to reason—right, Huey?

[*A beat.*]

STAGE MANAGER   All right, places—

MARTIN   We don't want to change you, son. We just want to change the people around you. I am thoroughly enjoying your program.

[SIMMONS *and* MARTIN *cross away.*]

DELRAY   Well, what the hell did you think was gonna happen?

STAGE MANAGER   And in four—three—two . . .

BOBBY   [*Into camera.*] And now boys and girls . . .

HUEY   Bobby, stop, stop! I got an important announcement to make! Boys and girls, don't adjust your television sets. What you see in front of you is not your parents. It's me: Huey Calhoun. And the reason I been dressed like this, well, it's a warning. If you don't listen to good music—this is gonna happen to you!

[*Music starts.*]

Time to tear down the house!

"TEAR DOWN THE HOUSE"

HUEY   THERE'S A PARTY GOIN' ON
IN THE BASEMENT,
THERE'S A PARTY GOIN' ON
ON THE ROOF.

THE KIDS ARE ALL PSYCHED,
THE PUNCH IS ALL SPIKED,
AND EVEN THE WATER IS ONE HUNDRED PROOF!
WE'RE GONNA TEAR!

DANCERS   TEAR!

HUEY   TEAR DOWN THE HOUSE, WE'RE GONNA
STOMP!

DANCERS   STOMP!

HUEY   STOMP UP THE FLOOR, WE'RE GONNA HAVE
US SOME FUN AND WHEN WE'RE ALL DONE

HUEY and DANCERS   WE'RE GONNA HAVE US JUST A LITTLE BIT MORE!

[HUEY *begins to strip.*]

SIMMONS   What's he doin'?

MARTIN   I think he's maybe taking off his clothes.

SIMMONS   Shit.

[*Dance break.* HUEY *strips down to his shorts.*]

DANCERS   YEAH!

HUEY   OH, WE'RE GONNA TEAR!

DANCERS   TEAR!

HUEY   TEAR DOWN THE HOUSE, WE'RE GONNA STOMP!

DANCERS   STOMP!

HUEY   STOMP UP THE FLOOR!
GONNA HAVE US SOME FUN AND WHEN WE'RE ALL DONE

HUEY and DANCERS   WE'RE GONNA HAVE US JUST A LITTLE BIT MORE!

[HUEY *tosses his pants at* MARTIN *and angrily walks off.*]

SCENE 6

Dressing room—backstage. Moments later.

    [FELICIA *is getting ready.* HUEY *enters, sipping a drink.*]

HUEY   Hey, baby .

FELICIA   I'm almost ready. Did you meet the man from the network, how's it going?

HUEY   Great. I'm givin' 'em a helluva show.

FELICIA   Really, I . . .

    [*Turns, notices.*]

How come you're not wearing pants?

HUEY   So the man from New York— the man from New York is mighty impressed. In fact, he said he wants to sign me right up.

FELICIA   Oh, I knew it!

    [*Kisses him.*]

I knew it, I knew it.

HUEY Now wait, wait—I don't think New York is gonna work out, though.

FELICIA What? But you said he wants to sign you?

HUEY Me, yeah. Everyone else, though, them he wants to be a little more—what's the word now? Oh yeah, white.

FELICIA Of course. Well, maybe it's something you should consider.

HUEY What?

FELICIA I'm just sayin' . . .

HUEY I'm just sayin' it's just as well. See, I been thinkin', I'm Memphis, right? And I'm happy here. We're happy here.

FELICIA We?

HUEY Yeah.

FELICIA BUT THE MAN SAID HE'S GONNA MAKE ME A STAR.

HUEY Well, he said that 'bout me, too.

FELICIA BUT YOU PROMISED YOU'D COME TO NEW YORK.

HUEY   Well, New York ain't ready for me.

FELICIA   WELL, IT SEEMS THEY'RE READY FOR ME.

HUEY   But you said you wouldn't go, not without ol' Huey.

FELICIA   You could come and find another job on the radio, or do your concerts.

HUEY   I got such big plans for you right here, baby!

"LOVE WILL STAND WHEN ALL ELSE FALLS" REPRISE

I WILL SEE YOU THROUGH.
I'LL BE THERE FOR YOU.
WE WILL ENDURE
WHAT LIFE HAS IN STORE.
LOVE WILL STAND WHEN ALL ELSE FALLS.

FELICIA   THE MAN SAID HE'S GONNA MAKE ME A STAR.

HUEY   So—they want to whitify my dancers, and I stand up to it—but you—

FELICIA   But me what?

HUEY   Well, since when did I get blacker than you?

FELICIA   Now you hold on! You've got choices in this world I don't, sugar. You get to be white whenever you want. I'm colored every time I step out my door. So don't come tellin' me that you're some kind of hero and I'm some kind of sell out fool.

[*She begins to exit.*]

HUEY   No, baby, wait, I didn't mean that.

[HUEY *grabs her hand.* STAGE MANAGER *enters.*]

STAGE MANAGER   Miss Farrell, you're on.

[STAGE MANAGER *exits.*]

HUEY   Let me prove how much I love you.

SCENE 7

The TV set.

[*Lights up on a silhouette of the* CAVALCADE DANCERS, *snapping their fingers. Tempo quickens as the* BAND *kicks in.*]

BOBBY   And welcome back to Huey Calhoun's Rhythm and Blues Cavalcade!

DANCERS   AIN'T NOTHIN' BUT A KISS
THAT SETS A GIRL ON FIRE

BOBBY   With today's fantastical guest–

[FELICIA *enters*.]

FELICIA   A SIMPLE LITTLE KISS
ALL LIPSTICK AND DESIRE

HUEY   Ain't she somethin', folks.

FELICIA   CAN YOU HANDLE THIS?

HUEY   Just the prettiest thing.

FELICIA   I SAID, CAN YOU HANDLE THIS?

HUEY   What man could live without her?

FELICIA   TRY AND HANDLE THIS
AIN"T NOTHIN' BUT A . . .

[*And* HUEY *kisses her.*]

[*Everything stops for a beat.*]

[DELRAY *moves toward them to break it up, but* FELICIA *quickly steps back. A couple of TV crew people rush off as* SIMMONS *rushes in.*]

SIMMONS   Cut! Cut the feed! Now!

STAGE MANAGER [*Into headset.*] Cut the feed—just do it!— and we're out!

SIMMONS How could you, Huey?!

HUEY Felicia—

SIMMONS You want to get us all killed?

DELRAY You stay away from her now!

SIMMONS You are through here, boy! Through!

HUEY Fine! I'm through here, but I'm the number-one man in Memphis! I can walk into any damn station I want!

SIMMONS Well, you go ahead and try! Maybe you were the first to play colored music for whites, but now everybody does it! Look around, you're nothing special anymore!

HUEY What're you talkin' about?! I started it all!

SIMMONS You're a rebel, and folks grow tired of rebels. You had your time, but time's up.

[*To the* DANCERS.]

Y'all get outta here now! Go on home where y'all be safe!

[*The* DANCERS *exit.*]

I gotta make some calls, see if I can't get the police down here to fend off—whatever the hell's comin'

[SIMMONS *exits.* FELICIA *and* DELRAY *begin to exit.*]

HUEY Felicia—

FELICIA How could you? How could you do that? For everyone in Memphis to see.

HUEY 'Cause I love you, baby, I love you more than anything. I wanted everyone to see.

DELRAY We gotta get outta here now, Felicia.

HUEY No, baby, stay, you know what ol' Huey's like.

FELICIA Sugar, there's nothing for you here no more. So come with me to New York.

HUEY What?

DELRAY Felicia.

FELICIA We could be on a train tonight. And tomorrow night, we could be in Coney Island.

HUEY You and me in Coney Island? How 'bout that?

[*A moment between them.*]

I—I can't, ya know. I just can't. Stay. Please.

FELICIA   Sugar?

HUEY   Yeah, baby?

FELICIA   I wish you hadn't done that.

[*A final moment between* HUEY *and* FELICIA. *She exits.*]

DELRAY   It's better this way. It is.

[DELRAY *follows* FELICIA *off.*]

[*Music starts.* ALL *exit, except* GATOR, BOBBY, *and* ETHEL.]

HUEY   What the hell's so special 'bout New York anyway? I'm gonna have another job by tomorrow.

BOBBY   Huey, Ethel, and me are gonna go out for some beers—

ETHEL   Come with us.

GATOR   We'll go down to Beale, no one'll bother you there.

[HUEY *shakes his head no.* BOBBY *and* ETHEL *exit.*]

"MEMPHIS LIVES IN ME"

HUEY THERE'S A TOWN THAT I CALL HOME,
WHERE ALL THE STREETS ARE PAVED WITH SOUL.
DOWN ON BEALE, THERE'S A HONKY- TONK BAR.

[DELRAY *crosses, carrying a suitcase.*]

HEAR THE WAIL OF A BLUES GUITAR.
HAVE A BEER AND DROP A DIME
IN THE BLIND MAN'S JAR.
THE BLUES SING SOFTLY IN THE AIR
LIKE A SUNDAY MORNING PRAYER.

[FELICIA *crosses, carrying a suitcase.*]

JUST ONE MORE DRINK
AND YOU'LL SEE GOD EVERYWHERE.
LIKE A SAD, OLD MELODY
TEARS YOU UP BUT SETS YOU FREE,
THAT'S HOW MEMPHIS LIVES IN ME.

[*Folks from* HUEY'*s life appear.*]

THERE COMES A TIME WHEN
MUDDY WATERS RUN ROUGH
THERE COMES A POINT WHEN
A MAN HAS HAD ENOUGH.

LIKE A FRIEND WHO ALWAYS
STANDS BY ME, YEAH,

FOLKS   BY ME!

HUEY   MEMPHIS KNOWS ME . . . MEMPHIS SHOWS
ME . . . HOW THIS LIFE JUST HAS TO BE . . .

I COULDN'T EVEN TRY
TO RUN AWAY, SAY GOODBYE
HERE I WAS BORN,
AND HERE IS WHERE I'LL DIE.

I'M JUST A MAN FROM TENNESSEE
CAN'T BE WHAT I CAN'T BE
ALL I KNOW IS MEMPHIS LIVES IN ME.
WOAH!

HUEY and FOLKS   [*With riffs.*] OOO . . . AHH . . . (WOAH,
WOAH, WOAH) OOO . . . AHH . . . WOAH . . . OHH . . .
OHH . . .

HUEY
THERE COMES A TIME WHEN
MUDDY WATERS RUN ROUGH
THERE COMES A POINT WHEN
A MAN HAS HAD ENOUGH.

LIKE A FRIEND WHO ALWAYS
STANDS BY ME, YEAH

MEMPHIS KNOWS ME
MEMPHIS SHOWS ME
HOW THIS LIFE JUST HAS TO BE.

I COULDN'T EVEN TRY
TO RUN AWAY, SAY GOODBYE
HERE I WAS BORN,
AND HERE IS WHERE I'LL DIE.

HUEY and FOLKS
JUST A MAN FROM TENNESSEE
CAN'T BE WHAT I CAN'T BE
ALL I KNOW IS MEMPHIS LIVES
ALL I KNOW IS MEMPHIS GIVES
ALL I KNOW IS MEMPHIS LIVES

HUEY   IN ME!

SCENE 8

A cramped, dingy radio station. It's four years later, but HUEY looks several years older.

[HUEY *at the mike. He smokes*]

HUEY   And this is Huey—comin' at you from WRKN . . . way, way up on the radio dial. And we just got the ratings in today and I ain't too good with numbers but seems we got ourselves about, well, one radio listener. Hello, one radio listener. Anyways,

I'm gonna play me one of my favorite records by someone who's startin' her very first nationwide tour tonight.

[*He plays* FELICIA's *recording of "Someday."*]

Oh, that's good. This—this music she sang, well, I always said there was somethin' special about it and I was the very first to play it in the center of the radio dial and everyone said, "Huey, you crazy" . . . Well, I guess the world can just go right on without you. Hocka damn doo.

[FELICIA *enters. She looks fantastic.*]

FELICIA   So my tour bus is pullin' into Memphis—

HUEY   Felicia—

FELICIA   And the driver's got the radio turned up to the edge of the dial—

HUEY   What you doin' here?

FELICIA   And I hear this funny voice that I haven't heard in, I don't know, four years? And the driver says he's listenin' to his very favorite station.

HUEY   He must be my one radio listener—

FELICIA   So I told my band—and they are very cranky—I told 'em I gotta make a little pit stop before we get to the Orpheum.

I hope you don't mind.

HUEY   Hell, I don't mind at all.

FELICIA   Yeah?

HUEY   Yeah.

FELICIA   It's good to see you. How you doin', Huey?

HUEY   Pretty good. I got me this okay little job.

[*Wiping the seat.*]

You wanna sit or somethin'?

FELICIA   I can't, everyone on the bus is waitin' for me. We're late for our sound check.

HUEY   Hey, why don't you come over for supper after the concert! Mama ain't gonna be home so . . .

FELICIA   Oh no, my fiancé is with me.

HUEY   Oh. I—I didn't know. Y'all happy?

FELICIA   We are, yeah.

HUEY   I'd like to hear more about him—

FELICIA   Well, his name is Bill . . .

HUEY   Okay, that's enough.

FELICIA   You got anyone?

HUEY   I got my music.

[DELRAY *enters.*]

DELRAY   Hey, uh, we really gotta get goin'—

HUEY   Hey.

DELRAY   Hey.

FELICIA   Just gimme one more minute—

DELRAY   You ask him yet?

HUEY   Ask me what?

FELICIA   One minute, okay?

[DELRAY *nods and begins to exit.*]

HUEY   Del—it's good to see ya.

DELRAY   Yeah. By the way, I really hate her new fiancé.

FELICIA   Get out.

[DELRAY *exits.*]

HUEY   Ask me what?

FELICIA   To come to my concert tonight. Gator said you weren't plannin' to but I wouldn't feel right being onstage in Memphis without you.

HUEY   No, I can't, I, uh, got plans.

FELICIA   No, you don't.

HUEY   Yeah, I don't.

FELICIA   Huey, you have to be there.

HUEY   Why?

FELICIA   'Cause I wouldn't be there without you.

HUEY   You mean that?

FELICIA   I do. Yeah. I do.

[*A beat. She touches his hand.*]

HUEY   Well, thanks, ya know, thanks, but . . . I can't get up on that stage. Ain't no one gonna remember me. They ain't even gonna remember my name.

FELICIA   So you tell 'em. You're Huey Calhoun.

HUEY   I was Huey Calhoun. What would I say to 'em all anyways?

"STEAL YOUR ROCK 'N' ROLL"

I LISTENED TO ADVICE
FROM FOLKS SMARTER THAN ME,
AND I IGNORED IT.

FELICIA   Yeah. Come to my concert.

HUEY   I LISTENED TO HATRED
FROM FOLKS RICHER THAN ME,
AND I DEPLORED IT.

FELICIA   You did.

HUEY   I LISTENED TO MUSIC
FROM FOLKS DARKER THAN ME,
AND YOU KNOW I ADORED IT!

FELICIA   Come to the concert, Huey—

HUEY   I don't think I can—

[HUEY *exits as the* BAND *appears and scene transitions into* FELICIA's *concert, with* BACK UP SINGERS *and* DANCERS.]

FELICIA   FIRST COMES A POINT IN EVERYBODY'S
LIFE,
WHEN THEY GOTTA STAND UP
AND FACE A FIGHT.
THEN COMES A POINT IN EVERYBODY'S LIFE,
WHEN THEY GOTTA WONDER
IF THEY DONE RIGHT.
I SWALLOWED MY FEAR,
FOLLOWED MY HEART RIGHT HERE,
AND THROUGH IT ALL
ONE ALMIGHTY THOUGHT STOOD CLEAR—
LISTEN TO THE BEAT
LISTEN TO THE BEAT
PLAY IT
OBEY IT
LOVE IT WITH
LOVE IT WITH YOUR FEET

[HUEY *enters. All stop for a moment, surprised he has come.*]

HUEY   OOOH, OH, OH, LISTEN TO YOUR SOUL,
LISTEN TO YOUR SOUL
HEED IT

FELICIA   HEED IT

HUEY   YA NEED IT

FELICIA   YA NEED IT
LET IT MAKE

ALL   LET IT MAKE YOU WHOLE

HUEY   AND IF YA LISTEN TO THE BEAT,
AND HEAR WHAT'S IN YOUR SOUL,
YOU'LL NEVER LET ANYONE
STEAL YOUR ROCK 'N' ROLL!

   [DELRAY, BOBBY, *and* GATOR *enter.*]

ALL   LISTEN TO THE BEAT, LISTEN TO THE BEAT

DELRAY   PLAY IT

ALL   PLAY IT

DELRAY   OBEY IT

ALL   OBEY IT

BOBBY   LOVE IT WITH

ALL   LOVE IT WITH YOUR FEET

BOBBY   GOTTA LOVE IT WITH YOUR FEET!

ALL   LISTEN TO YOUR SOUL, LISTEN TO YOUR SOUL

GATOR   HEED IT

ALL   HEED IT

GATOR   YA NEED IT

ALL   YA NEED IT

GATOR   LET IT MAKE

ALL   LET IT MAKE YOU WHOLE

HUEY   AND IF YA LISTEN TO THE BEAT
AND HEAR WHAT'S IN YOUR SOUL
YOU'LL NEVER LET ANYONE STEAL—

DELRAY   YOUR ROCK 'N' ROLL!

ALL   LISTEN TO THE BEAT
HEAR WHAT'S IN YOUR SOUL
YOU'LL NEVER LET ANYONE STEAL—

GATOR   YOUR ROCK 'N' ROLL!

ALL   LISTEN TO THE BEAT
LISTEN TO THE BEAT
PLAY IT

OBEY IT

FELICIA   LOVE IT WITH

ALL   LOVE IT WITH YOUR FEET

GATOR   GOTTA LOVE IT WITH YOUR FEET

BOBBY   LISTEN TO YOUR SOUL

ALL   LISTEN TO YOUR SOUL

DELRAY   HEED IT

ALL   HEED IT

DELRAY   YA NEED IT

ALL   YA NEED IT

GATOR   LET IT MAKE

ALL   [*With* FELICIA *riffing.*] LET IT MAKE YOU WHOLE
AND IF YOU LISTEN TO THE BEAT
AND HEAR WHAT'S IN YOUR SOUL,
YOU'LL NEVER LET ANYONE,
NEVER LET ANYONE,
NEVER LET ANYONE STEAL—

HUEY   The name is Huey Calhoun. Goodnight and hockadoo!

ALL   YOUR ROCK 'N' ROLL!

End of Show

ABOUT THE AUTHORS

JOE DiPIETRO (book, lyrics) won two Tony Awards—Best Book and Best Score—for *Memphis*. His Broadway show *All Shook Up* has had multiple tours and productions. His other musicals include *I Love You, You're Perfect, Now Change* (the longest-running musical revue in Off-Broadway history), *The Toxic Avenger* (with David Bryan), and *The Thing About Men* (both *The Toxic Avenger* and *The Thing About Men* won the Outer Critics Circle Award for Best Off-Broadway Musical). His plays include the much-produced comedy *Over the River and Through the Woods, The Art of Murder* (Edgar Award winner for Best Mystery Play), *Creating Claire*, and *The Last Romance*. His work has received thousands of productions across the country and around the world.

DAVID BRYAN (music, lyrics) won two Tony Awards—Best Score and Best Orchestrations—for *Memphis*, as well as Drama Desk Awards for Best Music and Best Orchestrations. He also co-wrote the award-winning musical *The Toxic Avenger* (with Joe DiPietro). David is the keyboard player and a founding member of Bon Jovi. He has won a Grammy Award and several American Music Awards. Over the past twenty-six years, Bon Jovi has sold more than 130 million records and continued to tour the world, playing to millions of people. David has done work for many charities, most notably as the national spokesperson for VH1's Save the Music Program, dedicated to improving the quality of education in America's public schools by restoring music programs in cities across the U.S.